SIGNS OF HOPE

IN A CENTURY OF DESPAIR

To

John R. Mott

who, in the darkness of our time,
has always seen light, and whose
life has made credible the faith that
the light is there

Contents

Preface

FOR A generation we have been familiar with the idea that we were at "the end of our time," that we lived "at the end of an era" that we existed "in the time between the times." Now, as we prepare for the second half of our century, there is a subtle change. We are beginning to catch advance rays of possible dawn, which give us some hint of what the new day may be. These hints come from the effectiveness and courage of minorities, but that is almost always the fashion in which creative forces appear.

We have had much intelligent and helpful diagnosis of our sickness, and latterly some minds have been seriously concerned with prescriptions for cure, but now we may take a third step and note some of the evidences of emergent health. The bombed out cellars are still representative of our time and constitute a continuing indictment against us, but some surprising flowers are beginning to grow among the rubble and the weeds. I am convinced that the majority of our people are almost wholly ignorant of the creative forces which are appearing at the middle of this century as genuine signs of hope in a time of general despair. In this book I have sought to analyze the subtle change that is occurring and to present some of the most important evidence concerning the nature of that change. It is my hope that the very recognition of what is going on may encourage others to try to have a share in it and possibly to enlarge it.

The thinking in these chapters has enjoyed, to an unusual degree, the immense advantage of a widespread ap·plication of the experimental method. Parts of it have been tried out, during the past academic year, on audiences of students and instructors in twenty-nine American colleges and universities. In every case the listeners have added something to the argument or to the evidence. Larger portions were used in the following conferences during the past summer: The Episcopal Conference at Cranbrook School, Michigan, the Auburn Week of Union Seminary, New York, the Pastor's Conference of Louisville Presbyterian Seminary, the Baptist Conference at Green Lake, Wisconsin, the Massanneta Conference in Virginia, the Institute of Theology at Montreat, North Carolina, and the School of the Prophets at Purdue University, Indiana. In all of these many thoughtful listeners made valuable criticisms that have led to numerous deletions and additions. Readers may now have the satisfaction of recognizing the thoughts which they so generously shared.

Before they were used in conferences the ideas expressed in these chapters were developed specifically for three named lectureships which I have had the privilege of holding in 1949. This book, therefore constitutes the Campbell Lectures of Sewickley, Pennsylvania, the Clark Lectures of Pomona College, California, and the Charles Wood Lectures of the National Presbyterian Church, Washington, D. C.

E. T.

Earlham College
Labor Day, 1949

SIGNS OF HOPE

IN A CENTURY OF DESPAIR

CHAPTER I

Half Past Nineteen Hundred

Only that day dawns to which we are awake. There is more day to dawn. The sun is but a morning star.

HENRY D. THOREAU

THE twentieth century has been a remarkably self-conscious century. As it opened there was a general conviction that it would be a truly new time, but there was no clear understanding of what its novel character might be. Now we are at its middle point and we are beginning to envisage, with some accuracy, its paradoxical nature. We now know that it is at once more sordid and more wonderful than any of the prophets of fifty years ago supposed it could be.

Of all earlier writers who sought to gauge the temper of the new time none is today more instructive than C. F. G. Masterman whose book, *In Peril of Change,* has a continuing fascination for those who once start to read it. Masterman's sensitive book appeared in 1913 when he had no intimation of the terrible upheaval which was to follow so suddenly and to continue so long. As he saw the new time with the spread of the white man's civilization and the advance of natural science he was deeply worried by the

general mood of tranquillity. Masterman was wise enough
to know that unpredictable events might take place and
the calm might be a calm before a storm, as indeed it was,
but he feared the tranquillity because he was sure that the
best elements of human life never appear under such circumstances. How incredibly remote do these 1913 sen-
tences now seem!

For the first time in many centuries, and especially in the
Anglo-Saxon world, in England, in parts of America, and in
the Colonies, we see a race developing who have experienced
nothing but a serene and ordered existence. From the beginning they have been sheltered from the disturbing elements
of life. They do not possess imagination necessary to realize
that this is an abnormal and transitory phase of the world's
development. All their accepted ideas in art, ethics, and religion, are inherited from times when this tranquillity was
lacking. They are becoming vaguely conscious that for them
the language is strained, extravagant, unreal. They have no
conception of the meaning of such a cosmic upheaval, the
disarrangement of a universe as, for example, the great dis-
turbance of '89 in France or the deliquescence of the whole
social order before the invader in 1870.[1]

We have every reason to believe that Masterman's sober
words were true when he wrote them shortly before 1914,
but there has not been a subsequent year when they were
true. For thirty-five years we have become increasingly conscious of "disturbing elements," of "cosmic upheavals" and
of the "disarrangement of a universe." In the conscious

[1] C. F. G. Masterman, *In Peril of Change* (New York: B. W. Huebsh,
1913), p. 167.

lifetime of most of us now living the ancient language, as found in tragic poetry and the Bible, has ceased to be "strained, extravagant, unreal," because modern events have made the strong language of an earlier day seem contemporary. We have had to learn to live, for thirty-five continuous years, in a mood of crisis. The consequence is that we are farther away from 1913 than we are from 586 B.C. or A.D. 410.

As the brilliant interpreter of the opening of our century of paradox saw it, even the perils of nature were rapidly diminishing. "There is," he wrote, "no fear of great epidemics." We hear, occasionally, of an earthquake or famine, but it is always something remote and consequently only partly believed.

The old fear—the panic fear—of some sudden menace no longer lurks in the shadows. The feelings of horror with regard to Nature and its operations and the feelings of insecurity are passing away from the minds of men. The general view of Nature which this new race is cultivating is that of the well-ordered watering-place which is the sole experience of most of them: a cleaned beach, breakwaters to temper the rough onslaught of the sea, with promenade and pier and safe playing-ground for the children.[2]

The great fear, forty years ago, was that this almost total absence of strain would remove from human life nearly all the sense of tragedy that has been man's highest glory. The very gospel, under such circumstances, becomes a mere gospel of decency and good manners, while any agony of

[2] *Ibid.*, p. 168.

soul appears to be pathological. The language of the ancient liturgies, a language wrung out of passion and terror,
seems archaic and consequently meaningless.

It was Masterman's terribly accurate prediction that such
a time of calm, with its attendant inability even to understand the great periods of human crisis, could not last. It
was, he said, transitory; it was only the *delusive* calm with
which the century of storm opened. "How the change will
come," said the essayist, "it is impossible to foresee. Perhaps
there may arise the sudden and unexpected outbreak of
forces fermenting among the neglected populations, of
whose existence and whose hunger for the material goods
denied them this ordered state has but little apprehension."

The first thirteen years of our century were calm indeed,
but there has been no calmness since. We have seen revolu-
tions greater than that of 1789 and we have seen invasions
which make the invasion of 1870 seem a friendly maneuver.
In our days we have seen the Russian Revolution, the rise
and decline of Fascism, the elimination of both Germany
and Japan as first-class powers, the fall of France, the formation of the United Nations, the independence of India, the
immense change in status of the British Empire, the Com-
munist victory in China, and the establishment of Pax
Americana over a great part of the Western world. In
addition to these has been the greatest scientific discovery
of human history. We have had countless problems to face
in our mature lives, but we have not had the problem of
moral lethargy arising from the elimination of dangerous
living.

Whatever our century may be, it is not the century of the

watered garden and the cleaned beach. It is the century of starvation, of concentration camps, of widespread famine, of unexampled terror. The vision of the cleaned beach with the breakwater was very remote to men who landed from open boats on the Normandy coasts. The people of bombed cities and the families of men who are still prisoners of war have experienced no overdose of tranquillity.

Now that we have had our thirty-five-year war, which gives every evidence of becoming a fifty-year war, we can hardly believe that thoughtful men once feared that life would become too calm. Instead of peace we have had continual violence, of one form or another, and more wanton cruelty than has been seen for generations. Instead of freedom we have experienced the rise of various systems of authority, both secular and clerical, and instead of security, there is endemic in the earth the mood of anxiety which expresses itself as an interim mentality. The century which was to have been too peaceful is one of unexampled storm and bids fair so to continue. The strong chance is that many of us now living must accommodate ourselves to the prospect of living all our days in the midst of strain. Just as the war which began in 1914 has not ended, but has only changed phase, so we may reasonably expect that the present tension, if finally overcome, will be succeeded by another. We have come into the stormy latitudes of history. There may be peaceful seas ahead, but the way to them lies through the stormy ones. The way of wisdom lies not in a refusal to understand these things, but rather in learning how to live in such cosmic weather. "Peace in our time" is a great dream, but we shall not see it.

If we get through this century, we may get through many more, just as America, if it could get through the 1860's, had a chance to go on for many subsequent generations. Our century lies in the equinoctial disturbances between the seasons when trouble is inevitable. That grave human difficulties should attend the coming of age of technology is in no way surprising. It is by no means certain that we can survive safely this intermediate period; a slight error in judgment might bring incalculable tragedy or total failure, but conversely, a series of right decisions might do wonders for mankind. Ours is a fluid time, but it will not always be so. As a result of our cumulative decisions now, the twenty-first century may be a new dark age, or it may be incalculably better than anything we now know.

Many of us who had our formal education in the early years of this century grew up with a profound sense of relief in the realization that we were fortunate to live in a time when the terrors of former centuries were unthinkable. We read of the persecution under Domitian or Nero and congratulated ourselves that this was all far away and long ago. We knew that America was founded, in large measure, by persons who sought to escape religious persecution in Europe, but it never occurred to us that we might live in an age of religious persecution of the most bitter sort. Our childish optimism seems strangely remote when we face the sobering fact that even now, long *after* the Nazi terror, Protestants of Spain are liable to arrest if they publish their teachings or even distribute Bibles. There was nothing inevitable about the human progress in which we once so easily and so uncritically believed.

The mood of our time is subtly marked, at all levels of

society, by a keen sense of disappointment, even though it is not always so expressed. Much of the basis of this disappointment is the vivid contrast between the promises and the fulfillments of our age. Never were promises so grand and never was the failure so apparent. Our people were oversold on what science and its technological products could and would do for mankind, but now even the dullest can see that these rosy promises have not been kept. One does not need to be a philosopher to realize that there can be bitterness in air-conditioned houses and that there can be gross injustice among people who go to the courtroom in fenderless cars. Even the unreflective must notice that trivialities are just as trivial when they are transmitted by the wonders of television.

The more thoughtful are beginning to suspect that there may be a genuine connection between our inventive cleverness and our human difficulties, in that the same techniques by which we have overcome the perils of nature have, by their very character, increased the perils of history. We have less reason to be frightened of flood and drought and ocean waves, but we have more reason to be frightened of our fellow men, and the fury of the elements is as nothing when compared with the fury of angry or fanatical men. "The increasing command over the environment which an ironic or malicious or retributive Providence is apt to bestow upon a society in disintegration only serves, in the end, to put a greater driving power into the suicidally demented society's chosen work of self-destruction."[3]

A dim realization of such matters, on the part of millions,

[3] Arnold Toynbee, *A Study of History,* Vol. V (London: Oxford University Press), 1946, p. 16.

has brought about the end of optimism. Whatever our age may be, it is not optimistic and cannot be. No living person is so blind as to suppose that things are naturally getting better and better. But it would be rash to suppose that the mood which follows optimism is necessarily a beneficent one. On the contrary the successor to easy optimism is often an ugly mood, as of people who half feel that they have been cheated. This is one of the reasons why the idealistic propaganda in the Second German War had generally a poor reception. It is also one of the reasons why authoritarian systems take hold of the public mind so easily; they demand no courageous act of faith.

Our people, conscious of being cheated, in that what they believed so naïvely failed to materialize, show many evidences of mental and moral breakdown. The recent study of mental illness in Kansas, as reported by the *Kansas City Star,* is so shocking as to be almost unbelievable,[4] but the trend it reports is substantiated elsewhere by the necessary enlargement of facilities for the care of the mentally ill. Add to this the sharp increase in the number of alcoholics and the enormous demand for books dealing with all forms of anxiety. The phenomenal sale of Rabbi Leibman's *Peace of Mind* reveals something important about our generation; it is the ill and not the whole who seek a physician. We can tell what people do *not* have by noting what it is that they seek frantically to secure. The growing popularity of Norman Vincent Peale's *Guide to Confident Living,* is an accurate index to the general absence of confidence. Our immensely lucrative entertainment business is

4 The report is that, in Kansas, one in ten needs mental hospital care.

likewise an accurate measurement, not of happiness, but rather of sadness and boredness.

Even our religion may provide numerous symptoms of decay. The crowds of people who gather to hear the various psychotherapeutic preachers give some notion of how many frustrated and confused people there are. The popularity of a book describing the experiences of a Trappist monk is chiefly instructive in that it indicates a mentality; it shows that thousands are tired of ordinary life and would like to find some escape, at least in their dreams. It is, however, very far from robust religion.

Though our colleges and universities have minorities of deeply concerned students, these are often made acutely conscious of the fact that they *are* minorities. In academic institutions from coast to coast the characteristic student has some scattered bits of knowledge and perhaps some skill, but there are thousands who have no conception of life's meaning or any encompassing purpose which can utilize the bits of knowledge and the skills. What is probably the majority of our more than two million young people in institutions of higher learning do not know even the rudiments of the Christian religion and have never heard it expounded in an intelligent or convincing fashion. They are illiterate concerning the roots of their own democracy. What is worse than a failure to achieve a sense of life's meaning is the fact that so many have no interest in the problem of meaning, and consider it very amusing that anyone should have such antiquated interest. A few would question Socrates if he were to come among us, but most would consider the discussion of the right and the good, the beautiful and the true as highly ridiculous if not downright neurotic. What they desire, and what they mean to get, is a good paying job, security and a late model car. The fear of countless undergraduates is the fear of seeming intellectual, a danger which they avoid at all costs.

We understand our temper with some accuracy when we see what will draw a crowd. Will the largest crowd appear for a modern saint and thinker like Albert Schweitzer? Certainly not. He drew a good many when he spoke at Aspen, Colorado, and at the University of Chicago, but he could not equal, in drawing power, a high school basketball tournament. Judging by the experience at the University of California the only speaker who can draw a larger crowd than is drawn by a university basketball game is Professor Kinsey. Others must be publicized, but his theme, whether it be the sex life of the American male or the sex life of the American female, seems to require neither explanation nor advertisement. This tells us something instructive, not about Professor Kinsey, but about our age. However eloquent the Indiana University professor may be, it is his subject and not his eloquence that draws the crowds. The subject would have been equally successful in drawing crowds in ancient Rome, especially in its period of decay.

With each succeeding week we are given new evidences of our inner decay. At one time it is the peddling of influence in Washington, the acceptance of expensive gifts by highly placed officials and the bland self-righteousness which says that there is no connection between such gifts and services rendered. At another time it is the outbreak of violence in protest against a meeting scheduled for the discussion of civil rights, a kind of violence amazingly reminiscent of Berlin street scenes in the 1920's. And all along we let potatoes rot in the field and are puzzled to know how to store our wheat crop, with the former year's crop still unused, while millions of God's children live at the starvation level.

In all this there is nothing new. This is not the first time that there has been a loss of moral nerve and it will not be the last. Similar and more extreme symptoms appeared in the ancient Graeco-Roman world and they evidently appeared in civilizations which have ceased to exist. That is the permanent significance of the story of Sodom and Gomorrah. Apparently these societies lacked even the minimum of concerned men necessary for survival. What is new is not the loss of a sense of meaning, important as that is, but rather the fact that this loss is synchronized with some external developments which are truly novel.

There have always, so far as we can observe, been dangerous and ruthless men, willing to destroy others if, by consequence, they might improve their own situations, but today such men can be incalculably more effective than ever before. For the first time in all history the entire population of the earth can be imperiled by ruthless men *at any point on its surface*. Every point on the earth lies within two days' travel of every other point. This is the only sense in which ours is "one world"; it is one in potential danger! The predicament of one group may, thanks to twentieth-century cleverness, be the predicament of all.

The second element of novelty in our contemporary historical situation is the present division of the world's population into two self-conscious and hostile camps. This is the first time that the world has been divided into two antagonistic and balanced parts. In our undeclared, but well-understood war, at the middle of the century, there are two spheres of influence and all mankind is gravitating to one pole or the other. The days when the late Wendell Willkie's book *One World* was selling in railway stations like a newspaper seem incredibly remote, because even the illiterate now know that what we have is two worlds on one planet. It is not new for the race to be divided, since it has never been truly united, but it is new for the world to be *bifurcated*. And *two* is the worst possible number of divisions. When there are only two, and desperate men come into power, incalculable harm may be done.

As we come to the middle of the century we realize that its great and lasting mark may be that of the planetary civil war. *The twentieth century is the century of the background, development and continuation of the Great Civil War*. Our problem is whether we can survive in such a time and how those things which make life good, in this or *any* century, can be maintained and passed on to our posterity.

Since we belong to the Anglo-Saxon tradition it may be instructive to look into that tradition and contemplate the great civil wars which both sides of the Atlantic community have suffered. The American Civil War was a terrible thing, for which we are still paying a heavy price in various forms of human sorrow, but we must admit that it was likewise a time of greatness. The sight-seer in Boston cannot but be moved by the bas-relief which faces the State

House and, as he sees it, he has some hint of how young people felt in 1861. Out of the gory conflict there arises ever higher the magnificent figure of Abraham Lincoln. The Civil War revealed and even heightened his heroic stature. It will generally be agreed that the cruel strife was the occasion for his utterance of the noblest words that have been fashioned on the continent of North America. "With malice toward none, with charity for all," do not constitute a justification of the war, but they do show that nobility appears most noble in tragic circumstances and that ours is the kind of world in which the best thoughts can come in worst times.

We are similarly encouraged as we study the Civil War of Great Britain which was raging three hundred years ago. As our Civil War, on an international scale, has come in the middle of one stormy century, the British Civil War, on a national scale, came in the middle of another. In terms of speed of transportation the planet is now smaller than Great Britain was then and is therefore a comparable unit, so far as human measurement is concerned.

The British Civil War, as we read about it from those who shared in it, was a time of terrible breakdown. As a famous plaque in Stanton Herald says, it was a time when all things sacred were "either demolished or profaned." Three hundred years ago, as the British people came to the middle of their century of storm, King Charles I had been executed and the fighting between the Royal and Parliamentary forces was fierce. Many schools were closed, cities were partially ruined and economic activity was at a standstill. The people and their leaders had no fear of too much tranquillity then. In their address to the People of England the Parliament said, in 1653, "We cannot but acknowledge that we are not yet at rest: nor can we believe we have yet enjoyed or seen enough to accomplish the ends of God."

This is part of the story, but it is not the whole story. The other side of the story begins to appear when we find this same seventeenth century denominated by the late Professor Whitehead, "The Century of Genius." Real as was the decay, the reforming developments were equally real. Right out of the confusion there arose strikingly creative movements of a spiritual nature, some of which flourish to this day, the best known and most honored being the Quaker Movement. Though the people of Britain's Civil War could not have believed it possible, their period is now studied as the flowering time of English religious prose. Neither could they possibly know the degree to which their time of storm was crucial in the development of modern science.

During Britain's Civil War, in the middle of the seventeenth century, the following men of genius, among others, were alive: John Milton, John Locke, Isaac Newton, George Fox, Jeremy Taylor, Richard Baxter, John Bunyan, Robert Boyle. Here are great men in letters, great men in religion, great men in philosophy, great men in science. When we see what a galaxy they make we realize the aptness of Whitehead's now famous phrase. It was, in very truth, a century of genius. What strikes us with permanent force is not the pain and confusion of the time, real as they were, but the fact that greatness was able to arise out of the very pain and confusion and bifurcation.

In fact it is difficult to avoid envy of the men of 1650. The great Descartes, the originator of modern philosophy, had just died and his words were available to all. Galileo's system of thought was becoming known and Milton had just become Secretary for Foreign Tongues in the new Council of State. Men *can* think good thoughts in bad times and perform good deeds when events are most calamitous.

The demonstration provided by civil war is not unique. One of the most secure of the results of Biblical scholarship in the last hundred years is the recognition that the very words of the Old Testament, which apparently seem greatest to most thoughtful persons, came out of the time of fierce calamity. It is now believed that the noble chapters of Isaiah 40-55 were written, not in the end of the eighth century B.C., but rather in the time of the Babylonian captivity, after 586 B.C. What they prove is that men can sing the Lord's song in a strange land. The captivity was a terrible time, for the life of refugees is always hard, but the world is such that greatness can arise in such periods as it is not likely to arise in peaceful times. Masterman was right in his main estimate. If the world becomes a garden of Epicurus we cannot expect nobility as a response and even the strong words of the older literature will lose their meaning, but we are in no danger of such a development now. We are in a time of strain and, if we make the proper response to it, it will be a time of greatness. Out of our planetary civil war, as out of two famous struggles in the history of Anglo-Saxon culture on two sides of the Atlantic, there may come a new burst of spiritual life that will constitute a genuine Reformation in our time. The Civil War reveals bigotry and terror, but it may also reveal glory.

That ours is a time of a possible new burst through the crust of history is more than a reasonable guess; it is actually beginning to be demonstrated in some areas. In no area is this clearer than in the field of religion. Though there is vast religious apathy on the part of the majority, there is intense activity on the part of a minority and it is such minorities that may be truly creative of the future. When we think of the names of the men who, near the middle of our century, have given their thought to the honest consideration of religious truth, we find a galaxy not unlike that of three hundred years ago. Not for at least a century has there been anything comparable to the contemporary virility in theology. Among the great names are the following: the late William Temple, who died during the Second War as Archbishop of Canterbury; the late Nicolas Berdyaev, long of Russia and later of Paris; the brilliant Swiss theologians, Karl Barth and Emil Brunner; the Scottish brothers, John Baillie of Edinburgh and Donald Baillie of St. Andrews; Dr. Albert Schweitzer of Africa, whose place in the affections of thoughtful Christians is unique; Paul Tillich and Reinhold Niebuhr, of Union Theological Seminary, New York; Jacques Maritain of France and America. This is only the beginning of such a list, but it is a very striking one and should be sufficient to alter the opinions of those who have supposed that vigorous religious thinking is something from a dim and distant past.

Out of the many signs of new life which are appearing in the midst of our world civil war, four of the most important will be presented in the following chapters. They are, in no sense, a denial of the facts of terror, of loss of faith and of moral decay. They are, instead, evidence that new life can spring up in the midst of the decay. And the new life may be remembered when the decay is forgotten.

CHAPTER II

The Rise of the Horizontal Fellowship

Almost incidentally the great world-fellowship
has arisen; it is the great new fact of our era.
WILLIAM TEMPLE

AS THE noble utterances of Abraham Lincoln arose
out of the tragic conflict between the North and
South and could not have been produced in calmer times,
equally noble utterances have come out of our time as
they could not have come in tranquillity. As long as the
English language is spoken, men and women will remember "their finest hour" and they will remember it because
an eloquent man, stirred to his depths by the crisis, was
able to express a commonly shared emotion in uncommon
words. The paradox is that men may remember the words
longer than they remember the deeds commemorated by
them. At Gettysburg Lincoln said, "The world will little
note, nor long remember, what we say here, but it can
never forget what they did here," but his humility made
him a bad prophet. The deeds of Gettysburg seem increasingly remote and the battleground is now a pleasant park,

but Lincoln's words are deathless. They seem just as vivid now as when he first spoke them near the Pennsylvania village. He said that the brave men living and dead had commemorated the spot far beyond his power to add or detract, but in this he was wrong. Actually he added immeasurably.

As the secular leader of the British government was able to express perfectly for millions, what they could not say for themselves, the spiritual head of the British nation was also fortunate in public utterance. William Temple was as well fitted for his great task as Winston Churchill was fitted for his. There is some justification in fact for the widespread belief that God raises up great men in time of critical need.

On St. George's Day, 1942, in the midst of the terrible conflict, William Temple was enthroned as the Archbishop of Canterbury. Because few men who have been elevated to the position of primate of the Church of England have come to this high office with finer qualifications, his enthronement brought general rejoicing, far beyond the borders of his native land. The occasion gave the new Archbishop a magnificent opportunity to address the listening world and he was clearly conscious of the grave responsibility this opportunity entailed. It would have been understandable if he had concentrated on the war then raging and on the issues relevant to it. Probably this was what was expected. But, though Archbishop Temple mentioned the conflict, and though he made his own position in regard to it clear, it was not of strife and danger that he chiefly spoke. He spoke, instead, of the movement for the reunion of Christendom.

That William Temple should use valuable time when the strife was hot and the outcome far from obvious to speak of the ecumenical movement will seem strange only to those unacquainted with his great mind. Personally, he supported the war and supported it *as a Christian,* he maintained, because he was convinced that a German victory, with or without fighting, would bring untold misery to the human race and make impossible the many things for which Christian men care. While he had great respect for Christian pacifists, his own leading was not in this direction. But he was keenly aware, at the same time, that the war, which he considered a grim necessity, could never serve as a redemptive or healing force. At best the outcome of the war, he believed, would be *negative.* The war effort might prevent an evil thing, but it was wholly incapable of producing a good thing. Accordingly, it was of paramount importance that there should be people, right in the midst of the negative struggle, who were beginning to concentrate on positive healing forces. Someday, he saw, though he never lived to see it, the war would be over and then much of human hope would depend upon movements of a redemptive nature already in being and capable at once of crossing enemy lines. His major confidence, therefore, lay in the growing ecumenical movement which seemed to him to be the most vigorous form that internationalism has yet taken. We sorely miss the leadership which William Temple would have given had his life been spared, but fortunately we have his words uttered in the midst of war.

As though in preparation for such a time as this, God has been building up a Christian fellowship which now extends into almost every nation, and binds citizens of them all together in true unity and mutual love. No human agency has planned this. It is the result of the great missionary enterprise of the last hundred and fifty years. Neither the missionaries nor those who sent them out were aiming at the creation of a world-wide fellowship interpenetrating the nations, bridging the gulfs between them, and supplying the promise of a check to their rivalries. The aim for nearly the whole period was to preach the Gospel to as many individuals as could be reached so that those who were won to discipleship should be put in the way of eternal salvation. Almost incidentally the great world-fellowship has arisen; it is the great new fact of our era.[1]

This brilliant insight into the organic relationship between the missionary movement and the ecumenical movement cannot be too often stressed. *The paradox is that Christian diffusion has led to Christian unity.* We established missions in Asia and Africa and in the isles of the sea, pouring out money and time for the sake of people whom the donors were destined never to see or know, and most of this prodigious labor was accomplished through denominational zeal. But once the far-flung missions were established much of the denominational emphasis was necessarily transcended. It takes no great sense of humor to see the absurdity of Southern Presbyterianism in North-

[1] William Temple, *The Church Looks Forward* (New York: The Macmillan Company, 1944), p. 2.

ern China or of Japanese Dutch Reformed Christians. The hard life, the fierce battle with paganism, made countless missionaries and converts realize that they were in a single struggle, with one faith, and that they had enlisted under the banner of One Lord. Ecumenicity became a fact before it was a doctrine. Consequently, some of the greatest pressure which has been put on Christians to form the World Council of Churches has come from what are called the newer churches. Their influence has been increasingly felt since the great missionary conference in Edinburgh in 1910 and was strikingly evident in the Madras Conference of 1938.

For many years Japan has seemed to us in Europe and America a foreign mission field. Christianity came relatively late to the Japanese people and, for a long time, grew very slowly, but now the Christian faith is making remarkable advances in that nation. The Japanese Christians, partly through the pressures of war and defeat, have achieved today a degree of unity that is sufficient to shame those on what we call the home field. One of the most vivid evidences of a unitary approach is the common effort to establish an International Christian University in Japan. The plans for the new institution are maturing with remarkable speed and, in spite of their impoverishment, the Japanese themselves have exceeded their announced goal by raising more than 150 million yen. The official report is that more than 99 per cent of this money came from non-Christians because they recognized the Christian basis of democracy.

One important thing to say about the ecumenical movement is that it is very new. We are so surrounded by it now that we tend to forget its novelty, but we get something of the true picture when we think of earlier days in this same century. Nearly all of this movement toward effective reunion has come within the memory of living men and most mature persons can easily remember a time when this influence was not, in their local circles, felt at all.

One convincing evidence of the novelty of the ecumenical movement is the popular reaction to the very word. Many people smile a bit when they hear the word "ecumenical" as though it is a barbarous bit of jargon, but the truth is that it is no more difficult than "economical" and really very similar. It is a perfectly good word, meaning roughly the same as catholic, but without the controversial connotations of that well-known word. All that the reaction to "ecumenical" means is that the idea for which it stands is new to most people. For the majority, apparently, the Church has meant the local unit or sometimes the denomination, but seldom has it meant, until in the recent past, the world-wide fellowship of all who own the Lordship of Christ, whether Greek or Roman, Catholic or Protestant, Fundamentalist or Liberal, clerical or lay.

We understand something of the wonder of our time when we realize that this movement is scarcely a generation old. The series of international gatherings, which culminated on August 23, 1948, when the World Council of Churches became a living fact, began at Geneva in 1920, and even if we include the International Missionary Conference at Edinburgh, that takes us back no farther than 1910. What this means is that a revolutionary Christian change has been occurring under our very eyes. "A world-wide Christian community is discovering its existence, and giving to that existence outward and visible signs," says one of our ablest interpreters. "A people of God is forming once more, seeing itself as one in time with that people of God to which, according to an ancient story strangely neglected, God once made promises for all time. The twentieth century can understand again words proclaimed by God at the beginning of that people's history."[2]

Much of the novelty has arisen from a new sense of the meaning of the Church and a recognition of the centrality of the idea of the Church, so far as the Christian gospel is concerned. Earlier it was fashionable for the religion of many intellectuals to be mere individualism, but a deeper understanding has made us realize that Christianity is by its very nature social. The fellowship is not an extraneous result or an incidental factor, but is, instead, essential to the entire conception. Once there were wiseacres who raised a feeble laugh by saying they believed in Christianity, but not in Churchianity, but their humor has lost its effectiveness because it is now so severely dated. A clearer understanding of the Christian enterprise and especially the study of Christ's method of continuing his work has made us see that a non-Church Christianity is contradiction in terms. The gospel comes by means of the fellowship, and, whenever it is understood, leads to the augmentation of the fellowship. This is the profound and enduring meaning of the precept that there is no salvation

2 Theodore Wedel, *The Coming Great Church* (London: S. C. M. Press, 1947), p. 24.

outside the Church. When this dictum is used with a narrow or sectarian meaning of the Church it is always vicious, but no such arbitrary limitation is necessary. *Extra ecclesiam nulla salus* is orthodox theology.

One measure of the comparative novelty of this emphasis in the modern world is Charles Clayton Morrison's Yale Lectures called *What Is Christianity?*[3] These lectures would have been simply curious a generation earlier. The point is made vivid when we compare Morrison's book with a book by the same title written by Professor Harnack of Germany. Instead of defining Christianity in terms of doctrine or moral teachings or social applications, the American ecumenical leader has defined our faith in terms of the ongoing divine society. We understand something of the change that has come in the literate mind when we note that this book is not shocking. That it would have been shocking to many a generation ago is well shown by the following trenchant statement from the pen of Canon Wedel:

To many modern Christians the very idea of catholicity has been utterly foreign—particularly if this idea carries with it the assumption that to be a Christian means, first of all, membership in a community. To be a Christian has meant for most Protestants almost anything but churchmanship. It has meant loyalty to ethical ideals; it has meant personal trust in God; it has meant discipleship of Jesus; it has meant individual walking in the fear of the Lord; it has meant devotion to the Bible. All of these are precious in Christian life. These convictions and experiences were shared in parish or local church. Fellowship has never been lost in evangelical Christianity.

[3] New York: Harper & Brothers, 1940.

Protestant practice has been far in advance of its ecclesiology. Yet is it exaggeration to say that most Protestants, if pressed, would have placed the idea of Church a distant second in comparison with the idea of personal commitment to Christ?[4]

Again, as in the case of the missionary movement, ecumenicity has come as a by-product. When we recover the glory of the doctrine of the Church, we soon realize that we cannot mean by it merely the little meeting house on the village green. When we use the grand word in the singular, rather than the plural, we are forced to mean the Church as "the mighty commonwealth of God, universal, holy, with a majestic history, with divine sanctions of its own superseding those of any fractional grouping."[5] It is too catholic to be merely Roman, too orthodox to be merely Greek, and too independent to be merely Protestant. To this great Church, which is the true Church of Jesus Christ, we can be loyal even though we are yet far from its visible embodiment.

What we need to make clear is that the acceptance of such ideas, especially in all levels of Protestantism, constitutes a revolution so great that it may be reasonably compared to the spiritual revolution of four hundred years ago. We are not lessening our personal loyalty to Jesus Christ, but what we see so vividly is that the only way in which Christ can be revealed now is through a beloved society. He cannot be revealed in the pages of a book, for that is too cold; he cannot be revealed in a doctrine for that is too abstract; he cannot be revealed perfectly in any

4 *Ibid.*, pp. 24, 25.
5 *Ibid.*, p. 25.

man as his vicar, for such a man is bound to share in the finite predicament; but he *can* be revealed in the loving fellowship of men and women who, as individuals, are weak and fallible. It is the togetherness that is the point of glory.

Many in our time are coming to have a new significance of the meaning of the communion of saints. This communion extends in time through all the ages and it extends horizontally now across all the barriers which man, in his littleness, has raised. Anyone who can truly sing, from the heart, "For all the saints who from their labors rest," has begun to understand something of both the mystery and the power of the Christian faith.

The outward evidences of the reunion of Christendom in our time are many and rapidly growing. The World Council of Churches combines, in federal union, more than two hundred denominations and representatives of fifty countries. We have seen in America the union of three powerful Methodist bodies into one and the union is already a proven success. We have likewise seen the union of the Evangelicals with the Reformed Church, and now this combination is about to make a further combination with the Congregational-Christians and together they constitute the United Church of Christ which leaves the door open to all who are ready to join. Like Abraham Lincoln they are willing to walk with any man going in their direction. We may be sure that these mergers are only the beginnings of a great movement in our century which will soon attain much larger proportions. It is rolling like the mighty Mississippi. Let it roll!

Important as these official mergers are and will become, there is, in being, an ecumenical movement of far greater potential significance. This is the horizontal fellowship which already exists and often exists most vividly in those groups which have had, as yet, no official mergers. Such a horizontal fellowship is made up of people in all denominations who have, as their specific and peculiar mark, the characteristic that they have more in common with those across the lines than they have with those within their own lines. Every great denomination has strains and conflicts within its membership and the general rule in Protestantism is that the struggles within a particular body are far greater than are the struggles *between* the bodies. In every national church there is emerging a highly influential group, the real leaders, whose words sound almost exactly like those of the influential leaders of supposedly competing churches. The truly influential Baptists sound amazingly like the influential Presbyterians.

Earlier in our century the horizontal fellowship was comparatively small. Once Methodists read chiefly Methodist authors, and others did likewise, but that day seems to be permanently gone. Now we are in a day when *all read all*. The average literate Methodist will read, in a given year, more books by non-Methodists than by his own denominational exponents and interpreters. The same is true of Episcopalians, Baptists, and many more. Seldom do we ask what the particular sectarian background of an author is because nobody cares. We are more concerned with the product than with the label. When we read John Woolman's *Journal,* the primary fact is that he was a saint, while the fact that he was a Quaker saint is secondary. Sainthood cannot stay within a fence.

In our colleges where we seek the best interpretations of the gospel that are available, regardless of denominational affiliation, about the only valid criticism the students ever make is that all the speakers, regardless of denomination, say the same thing. The validity of this criticism is a tremendous ground of hope. When we deal with a certain level of concern, there is no way to separate devout Christians, unless we are given the labels in advance.

Whatever happens to the official movements in the direction of reunion, this living fellowship, to which many of the readers of this book already belong, is destined to grow. If it grows sufficiently the question of official union will be a secondary one, because the real unity will already be occurring.

In honesty, we must admit that this movement in the direction of Christian union in our time is by no means universal. There are Christian bodies who will have no part in it and some who look upon this development as just another evidence of decay. Not all Protestant bodies have united in the World Council and not all are willing to join, whatever the basis of unity may be. The Russian Church, among others, was conspicuously absent from Amsterdam and some of its members denounced the entire undertaking as a bourgeois plot.

The greatest chasm which still exists in the body of Christ is that between the Roman Catholic and all other forms of Christianity. The difficulties here are so great that, humanly speaking, we can see no light on the problem and no probability, in the foreseeable future, of a healing of this major breach. The difficulty lies in the fact that the Roman hierarchy declares itself unable to meet others on a basis of Christian equality, since the Roman Church is, by definition, the one true church and all others are in error. The Church of Rome is declared to be the one and only successor of the early Christian community and, therefore, the only possible basis of union is for all others who love the Lord to see the error of their ways and return to Rome. This is the reason why Rome was as conspicuously absent from Amsterdam as Moscow was.

Though we do not see any light on this terrible problem, this does not mean that there is no light to be seen. Humanly speaking, there seems to be no way, but, divinely speaking, there may be a way. Christ who said, "Other sheep have I which are not of this fold," may find a way to bring all into one fold. Difficult as this necessarily seems to us now, we must admit that our century has already seen developments which are almost equally surprising and which, in advance, were wholly unpredictable. We serve a Lord who said, "Other things have I to reveal to you, but ye cannot bear them now."

There are some who, in the fresh realization of the glory of ecumenicity in our age, jump to the conclusion that denominational loyalty is something to be renounced. Such a conclusion shows a superficial understanding of the movement which William Temple termed the great new fact of our era. Actually there is no conflict at all between denominational loyalty and ecumenicity and anyone who supposes there is a conflict has failed to understand one or the other. Indeed the chief way in which most of us can serve the Church Universal is by serving the particular church in which we have been reared or which we have later joined.

The most important reason for our loyal service to the tradition which is ours is that we hold some contributions in trust, not for ourselves, but for the entire Church of Christ and for mankind as a whole. If a Lutheran ceases to keep alive the great contributions which stem from Lutheran theology and practice, he is helping to cheat the universal church. He should keep certain practices going, not for the sake of Lutherans, but for the sake of catholic Christianity. The main tragedy of division and separation is that each section is poorer for its failure to have learned from those bodies of Christians from which it is separated. The Roman Catholics could profit immensely from the Quaker practice of silence, which is very different from that of the mass, and the ordinary Protestant could profit immensely from the Roman insistence on discipline. The task of each is to see that the others are not cheated by allowing some important facet of Christian truth to be lost or forgotten.

A Christian who has caught the vision of one Shepherd and one sheepfold has a threefold responsibility. For the sake of the total divine society he must, first, cultivate to the full the unique contribution which his group has to offer. Second, he must see that this contribution is made available to others in ways that they can understand and in a form which they can appreciate. These two responsibilities, if adequately met, serve to avoid the tragedy of waste. It would be a great shame for people who know so little and whose human vision is so dim, to miss any of the brightness which might conceivably guide them on their way. The third responsibility is that of listening attentively and open-mindedly to others, willing to receive as well as to give.

One of the marks of the thoroughness with which Archbishop Temple faced the problem of reunion is the fact that he did not allow his ecumenical enthusiasm to hinder, in any degree, his loyalty to the tradition in which he had been reared and in whose system he was so eminently fitted to serve. In his enthronement speech he made clear his double loyalty and his insistence on their full compatibility.

But we, who are assembled here, are not only individuals offering our service to the world-wide fellowship of Christian disciples, we are—with some honored guests representing the wider fellowship—members of the Anglican Communion, met in the Mother Church of the Communion, to set in St. Augustine's seat one more in the long line of his successors. We shall impoverish our service of the wider fellowship if we let our membership of our own Communion become hesitant or indefinite. Rather we have to make strong the bonds of our own unity, with gratitude for our splendid inheritance, so that we may bring to the universal Church a life strong in faith, in order, in corporate devotion—maintaining all that we have received but recognizing also God's gifts to His people through traditions other than our own.[6]

Here is true intellectual grandeur! This combination of catholicity with particularity takes us to an entirely dif-

6 *The Church Looks Forward,* pp. 4, 5.

ferent level from that demonstrated by the sectarian, whatever he calls himself, who supposes that his tradition is the only valid one, and also from the abstract Christian who is so loyal to the Church Universal that he forgets to support the particular church which is his only practical means of approach to the ideal. Temple was saved from the heresy of the right and from the heresy of the left. He knew that the dangers of broadness are quite as great as are the dangers of narrowness. A man may become so broad and tolerant that he has no message at all. This is what Temple had in mind when he said, on July 19, 1943, "The united Church must bring together all the elements of truth in all the several traditions, each unblunted as regards its definition and consequently as regards its cutting edge."[7] In the divine ordering there are many candlesticks, but all come from one stem. The light from the seven-branch candlestick is brighter and better than is the light from a single candle. The sacred responsibility of each part of the entire Christian fellowship is, while profiting from the lights of others, to see to it that one particular candlestick is not removed out of its place. This was the famous prayer of Lancelot Andrewes at the beginning of the seventeenth century, but it has equal significance today.

There is a conceivable kind of unity which is based on the meager uniformity of the least common denominator. This would be dull, indeed, and, moreover, it would be lacking in power. It would be hard to become enthusiastic or excited about such a prospect. There is, however, another ideal and that is the pooling of rich resources. The

7 *Ibid.*, p. 31.

result is not the dull monotone, but the brilliance of the patchwork quilt or the beauty of the mosaic. This alternative approach to unity was ably demonstrated at Amsterdam in the arrangement of the public services of worship each morning in the Koepelkerk of the Dutch city. Conceivably it would have been possible to work out a fairly innocuous service which would have hurt nobody's feelings, but which nobody would recognize as either his own or another's. Fortunately the organizers of the Assembly hit on a far grander, but equally ecumenical plan. Each of the morning services was different because each was in line with one of the constituent traditions of the Assembly. On one morning hundreds of all faiths shared joyfully in a Methodist service and on another morning the same people, for the most part, shared in a Congregational service. They were very different, partly because one was led by a bishop from St. Louis while the other was led by a Negro woman who now lives in West Africa.

This richer form of ecumenicity was sufficiently bold in conception to include even a Quaker meeting, though it was recognized that the Society of Friends is numerically infinitesimal. This Quaker meeting was held in strict accordance with ancient practice as developed so powerfully in the middle of the seventeenth century and no compromise was made in the light of the fact that the great majority of attenders were sure to be unfamiliar with this simple form of worship. Compromise was a temptation, in view of the obvious dangers involved, but, fortunately, the temptation was resisted. The result was that hundreds enjoyed what was for them a new kind of experience and a most rewarding one. They saw that the unity of the mosaic may be as genuine as the unity of the monotone wall. *E pluribus unum* is a live possibility. The many do not deny the one, nor does the one deny the many.

We understand better the absence of conflict in the two loyalties if we consider the American federal system. There is no contradiction in being both a good Hoosier and a good American. Loyalty to the welfare of Indiana is the most potent and practical form that the American loyalty of the average Hoosier can ordinarily take. In a larger way it is wholly possible to be a good Canadian and a loyal supporter of the British Commonwealth of Nations. Loyalties are compatible when they exist at different levels and this is the situation in regard to ecumenical denominationalism. The example of foreign missions makes this clear. We can raise millions more dollars for foreign missions if we raise this money as Methodists and Baptists and Lutherans than could possibly be raised on an undenominational level. This is simply a fact and there seems to be no good reason why the children of light should be more stupid than are the children of darkness. Many enterprises, such as publications, home missions, and youth work, can be carried on more vigorously on the denominational level. Let us, therefore, thank God for denominations and urge loyalty to them, *provided*—and this is a large provision—they envisage the validity of other approaches than their own. The logical danger is that we may draw negative conclusions from positive premises. The Baptist polity has im-

mense advantages, but it would be most illogical to con-
clude from this fact that the Presbyterian polity *lacks*
advantages.

There is a still deeper reason for thanking God for the
existence of the denominations. It has been fashionable, in
some circles, to criticize the Reformation to the extent of
wishing it had never occurred, or holding that its occur-
rence was a mistake, but such a judgment calls for further
analysis. Actually what the Reformation did was to apply,
in the development of the Christian faith, the principle of
the experimental or laboratory method. Nearly all the
main possibilities of Christian worship, Christian discipline and Christian polity have been tried and the consequence is that we now know much better what each possibility entails. It was not possible, in advance, to see,
precisely, the gains and losses of a system in which all ministers are equal, but Presbyterianism has provided, for almost
four centuries, a laboratory test. It was not possible, in
advance of experience, to know what would eventuate if
Christians should undertake seriously the abolition of the
laity, plus complete equality of religious opportunity for
women as well as men, but we now know something about
this, because the Society of Friends has given a demonstration of it for three hundred years. What happens if you try
out a bold independency, so far as the local worshiping
group is concerned? We need not wonder; we can ask the
Congregationalists and the Baptists, for they have tried it.
What happens when, with the use of the common language
of the people, you seek to keep the ancient continuity of
liturgical prayer? We need not wonder, for we can ask the

Anglicans and Episcopalians. And so it goes for Lutherans and Roman Catholics and as many more.

We cannot insist too strongly that the Reformation was a notable gain for the human race. Like any great movement, it involved a necessary price, but the dividends have been great. The effect on the political life of the world, in the production and encouragement of democracy has been prodigious. The monolithic Christianity of the Middle Ages cannot compare with the freedom and variety of the multiple composition which has come in post-Reformation times. Few pieces of nonsense are more nonsensical than the fashionable and sentimental glorification of the thirteenth century.

According to scholasticism experiment is not necessary; you merely think and speculate and then you know. But the mood of the modern world has renounced this arid system in favor of the experimental mood of science which *tries*. Do you want to know about falling bodies? Very well, drop the objects from the Leaning Tower and find out, said Galileo. Do you want to know whether a hybrid that is not sterile can be produced? Try it. To an amazing degree modern Christianity with its proliferation of movements has been in this stream of history. It has not all been gain, but sometimes the gains have been enormous. If now, without despising our ancestors or losing the real gains thus made, we can consolidate our gains in such a way that all can truly learn from all, ours will be a great day indeed. Our experiments which have often been conducted with such pain and against great opposition, will not have been in vain.

The great Christian movement of three hundred years ago was a movement of proliferation and fragmentation. That was the form their vigor took, a form so repulsive to some observers that one contemporary historian wrote a book about it and called it *Gangraena*. Now we are in a different kind of age, an age in which the characteristic religious developments are centripetal rather than centrifugal. Our problem is to see that we match our ancestors in virility and courage while we engage in what seems to be a radically different process. It is not necessary to renounce what they did. If we believe that the time has come for consolidation this does not mean that we despise in any sense the movement in the direction of experiment and exploration. Both are good, but there is a time for each. Ours seems to be a time of increasing unity and it is appearing most vividly when the sky is dark politically. The high hopes of secular union of the nations have been much dimmed since the enthusiastic meeting in San Francisco in the summer of 1945, but the prospects of the reunion of Christendom have not dimmed; they have, instead, become brighter as the dark century has advanced.

CHAPTER III

The Vitality of the New Theology

Theology is again a masculine discipline.
T. S. ELIOT

WE LIVE in a time when theology has been able to attract so many virile minds that even those who have tried to ignore theology are beginning to find it difficult to maintain their pose. The first and only visit of Albert Schweitzer to America was big news, even for the secular press, and the face of Reinhold Niebuhr has appeared on the cover of *Time,* along with business leaders and statesmen. The rank and file of our population may not have any clear idea of what the religious thinkers are saying, but they have a dim and growing consciousness that something is being said. What is it that is being said? Let us see.

The modern chapter in vigorous religious thinking took definite shape about a quarter century ago with the publication of a number of deeply moving volumes, among which were Berdyaev's *The End of Our Time,* Schweitzer's *The Decay and Restoration of Civilization* and Niebuhr's *Leaves from the Notebook of a Tamed Cynic.* Something of the impact of the mind of Karl Barth had already been felt in the Anglo-Saxon world, and though the majority of ministers and laymen were still innocent of the new forces the minority which began to feel them had unmistakable vigor and have now, after twenty-five years of thought and experience, put their mark on the mind of contemporary man in a most striking manner.

No summation of these new tendencies is likely to be complete, but just as a map helps us to find our way, even though it leaves out much of the detail of the countryside, so a brief analysis of the most interesting modern developments in theology may help the lay reader to see where he is going. Having employed the map to start he can then explore the terrain for himself.

The first great emphasis of the new theology of the second quarter of the twentieth century has been a renewed realism about man's nature. The movement has synchronized with a kindred movement in philosophy called "Philosophical Anthropology." For many reasons there has been a serious and concerted effort to study man's essential structure, his place in nature, his relation to the animals, his uniqueness, if any, his necessary limitations and his possible glory. In the modern world man has been a problem to himself to a most intense degree and this interest is reflected in many philosophical titles, the characteristic one being *Das Stellung des Menschen im Kosmos*.[1] It is probable that man is at least unique among the animals in that he alone is concerned with the problem of his own uniqueness. It is doubtful if the other creatures are concerned with theirs. Man may be, as has been alleged

[1] By Max Scheler.

in the past, the tool-making animal, the inventive animal, the laughing animal, but there is no serious doubt that he is unique in that he is the metaphysical animal, deeply interested in the problem of his own being. Whatever else he is, he is self-conscious, and from his self-consciousness arises much of his terrible danger as well as his potential glory and the very possibility of moral experience.

Philosophical anthropology was quickly matched by theological anthropology, with the result that no phrase has been more common among the galaxy of great names than "the human situation." The fundamental insight is that the predicament of man is essentially chronic and therefore continuous because man carries within himself the seeds of his own pain and sorrow. For men of the theological depth of most of those whose names have been mentioned in these pages the disappointments of the modern scene were not at all surprising and were, indeed, expected. They were expected by Christian thinkers because the Christian faith, when it is true to itself, has a realistic estimate of man which includes the conviction that whatever man does, he does as a *sinner*.

One of the first to make this emphasis abundantly clear in our Anglo-Saxon tradition was T. E. Hulme whose early death cut off what appeared to be the beginning of a brilliant intellectual performance. His book *Speculations* was, for the most part, ahead of its time and introduced a number of intellectuals to the doctrine of original sin. This ancient doctrine was supposedly well known, but the general view was that it was something believed only by obscurantists and persons of ignorant faith. Soon men of the

intellectual and cultural stature of T. S. Eliot were pre-
senting it as an intelligent and highly sophisticated approach to the mystery of man's soul.

We can understand this modern estimate of man's nature
and its inherent limitations more clearly if we see it as a
reaction to the optimism of eighteenth-century philosophy,
especially as represented by the school of Rousseau. This
optimistic theory is the notion that man is intrinsically
good and that he would *be* good were he not continually
corrupted by the social order. Man, if he were unhampered
by society, would be lovely and pure. Since he is harmed
because he is in an evil environment, his salvation lies
simply in emancipation from that environment. It is
obvious that this has been the actual metaphysical basis of
the work of many reformers in the last hundred years,
especially in social work and in some forms of education.
Nearly all of what is termed "progressive education" has
this as its actual metaphysical basis.

Now the new realistic theology attacks this optimistic
conception at all points. The Rousseau doctrine seems un-
critical and naïve to those who observe that man makes
society as truly as society makes man. What is most of this
hampering environment but the production of human
minds? The noble savage theme, though still attractive to
Hollywood, has no basis in fact, for people are not virtuous in proportion to their primitivism. The savage is not
really noble; in most instances he is merely dirty and even
more harassed by irrational fears than is the average city
dweller of the Western world. Albert Schweitzer's reports

on the natives of Africa, whom he has served for thirty-six years, are most illuminating on this point.

The optimistic theory was a great spur to the production of new idealistic or Utopian communities so many of which were started in the nineteenth century. An earlier version of the idea was influential in the original settlement of America, but the discouraging fact of history is that the new colonies soon began to exhibit many of the evils of the environment they had supposedly escaped by starting afresh. The most highly admired of all the early settlements of America, that of William Penn on the banks of the Delaware, was undertaken as "An Holy Experiment in Government," but before many years the holy experiment had descended to the level of extremely human controversies and struggles for power.

Though the history of other times has been eloquent on this point, it is the events of our own tragic century that have been most effective in blasting the notion of natural human goodness. We have had a revelation of the depths of wickedness in the human heart that makes naturalistic optimism seem particularly nonsensical. The war revealed aspects of human life that we had supposed, in our innocence, had been outgrown by the human race. The men who, in the nineteen twenties, published the theory of the awful wickedness of the human heart were provided, in the nineteen thirties and subsequent years, with a terrible verification of their words.

The doctrine outlined by the young Hulme and developed by T. S. Eliot and others is sometimes called "original sin," but we need not be bothered by the connotations of that disputed and much-misunderstood phrase. A far better term is "chronic sin" or "indigenous sin." The point is that man is, *qua* man, a sinner, even in his virtue. He may be able to overcome or to hold in check the sins of the flesh, but his temptations will not end thereby. In fact all agree that the sins of the spirit are far more terrible than are the sins of the flesh. Many persons who are not guilty of fornication or gluttony, and who may actually have no serious temptations in these directions, may develop sins of the spirit that are far more damaging to themselves and others than these can ever be. They may seek to destroy reputations and to spread slander; they may struggle cruelly for position and power. It has often been noted that such sins sometimes appear vividly among prominent churchmen, who may be truly ascetic in their physical existence, but absolutely ruthless in seeking to dominate others. Even the occupant of a monastery, far from the big noisy world, may demonstrate the subtler sins in really terrible ways. Of all the sins that of spiritual pride is probably the worst and the most damaging. It is thus that Paradise is lost.

It is largely because of a widespread return to the message of the Bible that so many Christian thinkers have been able to avoid the naïveté of characteristic secular thinkers in regard to the anthropological predicament. The Bible is a record of God's unique dealings with men, but it is not, for the most part, a book about good men. It is chiefly concerned with evil men and with a remarkable collection of evil deeds, as well as divine judgments upon those deeds.

Far from making men think that they are naturally good, it is the Bible which teaches men that all our righteousness is filthy rags. Disloyalty came even in the beloved society of the chosen twelve, the salt of the earth, and St. Paul wrote some of his epistles because of Christian squabbles.

A recognition of ugly facts like these is now general in our theological seminaries, but it has not always been so. Some indication of the crucial change that is occurring is provided by even a cursory study of Bible-school lessons and materials. The theological lag has been so great in some circles that the entire Biblical teaching, in so far as church-schools are concerned, is still that of sweetness and light. The children are told about birds and flowers and small animals, but they are shielded from the more bitter aspects of the Biblical message and sometimes have almost no teaching that is uniquely Christian. The kind of religion which such teaching produces may be charming, but is largely powerless, and does not fit people for the tragic world in which they are to live. One of the signs of health, however, has been the widespread revulsion against such a falsification of the faith, a revulsion that is becoming effective.

Sometimes, in our insatiable desire to put intellectual positions into labeled pigeon holes, this emphasis is called neo-orthodoxy, but we cannot too strongly emphasize the fact that the emphasis under discussion is far more widespread than is the influence of any one school, party or sect. It is, instead, part of the entire modern Christian mood. Note, for example, the realism in this matter shown by Harry Emerson Fosdick, who is far from being a

Barthian in theology. Because of his deep understanding
of the message of the Bible he was not gullible about the
war bringing peace. He knew that human sin, balked in
one place, would exhibit itself in another. Preaching at
Riverside Church, in the midst of World War II, he said:

When this conflict is over and its immeasurable sacrifices
have been poured out, Hitler, to be sure, will be gone, but
the basic problems that confronted us before even the fear of
totalitarian dictatorship, will confront us still, and endless
new problems as well that the war itself has caused.[2]

Another evidence that this kind of realism is not con-
fined to one theological party or tradition is shown in the
thinking of Bishop Francis McConnell, who, on the completion of twenty-five years of work as a Methodist bishop,
predicted that there would come soon a terrible outburst
of violence. At that time he had never heard of Mussolini,
but he did not need to hear of Mussolini; he studied a
book that told about Nebuchadnezzar and about Nero. At
the same time the current secular mood was one of almost
unconditional optimism. Perhaps it is the rôle of the Christian faith always to be slightly out of step with the world.
When the world is discouraged the Church must point to
the light that shines in the darkness.

Not only does the Bible tell, for the most part, about
sinners; it reserves some of its strongest denunciations for
those who suppose they are *not* sinners. We can never get
away from the terrific impact of the parable spoken by
Christ in which he contrasted the self-righteous man, who

2 Harry Emerson Fosdick, *A Great Time to be Alive* (New York: Harper
& Brothers, 1944), p. 1.

thought he had arrived, with the poor publican who realized keenly and sorrowfully that he had not arrived. It was the publican and not the Pharisee who left the temple justified. Though the Bible urges us on to perfection it gives no encouragement to suppose that perfection is achieved. Of this we may be sure: *a man who thinks he is righteous is not righteous*. And he is not righteous for the reason, primarily, that he is full of spiritual pride, the most deadly form that sin can take.

The early stories of Genesis, with which our Bible opens, are mostly fairly sordid tales of human failure. Sin, from the first, instead of being cured by knowledge is intrinsically linked with knowledge. The most revealing illustration of the classic human predicament is provided by the story of the flood. Since the world was evil, the sins of man were many, the social environment was bad and the theory that the evil was purely environmental was tested. God destroyed the social environment and left one comparatively righteous man, the best there was, to start the holy experiment over again. What a grand chance it was! The old cities with their vice were wiped away, the old external temptations were gone, so that Noah and his family could start freshly in a brave new world. Here was Rousseau's paradise if there ever were one. But what was the result? The Bible with its incisive realism shows that the first major act of Noah in his glorious new and unspoiled world was to get drunk! Romanticism simply is not true. Man carries the seeds of his evil in him and will carry them into any situation in which he enters, no matter how ideal.

This means that, if we are wise in the Christian sense, we do not expect Utopia. Hundreds of years from now our descendants, if there are any, will be facing difficult times and some of their worst problems will be the same old problems that plague us, just as our worst problems are the same ones that plagued Abraham and Confucius and Plato. This does not mean, of course, that we should, for this reason, cease to try to make the world relatively better. A philosophy which cuts the nerve of moral effort is an evil philosophy and this is what is evil in either sheer optimism or sheer pessimism. The sheer optimist has no incentive to struggle because, according to his view, things will get better inevitably anyway, and the sheer pessimist has no incentive to struggle because, in his view, nothing that he does will make any improvement. Men do not struggle to avoid or to produce that which they consider inevitable.

There is a third philosophy that keeps an incentive to struggle at the same time that it recognizes that Utopia will not appear. Though no complete solution of our human problems will ever come, so long as we are in our chronic predicament, there are some approaches to the problems that come nearer to the center of the difficulty than do others. We shall not make a perfect society in the next century or in the next millennium, but this is no excuse for failure to do our best to create an order relatively better than the confused and frustrating one in which we now live.

It is important to stress the fact that Christian thinkers have been, on the whole, ahead of their secular contemporaries and have, accordingly, been saved from a great deal of delusion by virtue of the Christian estimate of man's nature. Remembering the story of the flood, they did not expect new social experiments to exhibit the characteristics of the Beloved Society. They were very sure that the old human evils would appear in new economic settings as truly as in the old. This saves us from the gullibility of scientism, the notion that if only we can have enough science we shall have a good world. Scientists can be sinners as are other men and there is nothing in the nature of the human situation to keep them from prostituting their science. Even more the Christian estimate saves us from an easy belief in a technological heaven. Men may be as vicious with chromium fittings as in cabins, while neon lights are not likely to make men more virtuous than are kerosene lamps. We have, in America now, a good many communities which are practically ideal so far as material advantages are concerned. They have been able to take advantage of what technology can do, from air conditioning to vitaminized foods in any desired quantity. But since these ideal communities are inhabited by men and women they are often scenes of tragedy. Murders occur in tiled bathrooms as easily as anywhere else.

It is this same realistic estimate which, if we take it seriously, saves us from gullibility about the communistic or other leftist experiments. There are always some affinities between Christianity and communism and the early Church practiced sheer communism for a while, though the Bible tells us that it eventuated in the scandals of Ananias and Sapphira. No matter how idealistic is the initial movement which seeks to balance opportunities by breaking up the great estates of the absentee landlords and giving the land to the people, we ought to see in advance that the very leaders of such a leftist movement would soon be open to all the temptations of power which their capitalistic predecessors knew. The temptations of Stalin are similar to those of the Czar, as the temptations of an archbishop are similar to those of a civil ruler. Often these temptations have little to do with money, but much with prestige. The labor movement has undoubtedly been a necessary step in our contemporary life, but a Christian estimate makes us realize in advance that labor leaders will develop their own vested interests and engage in struggles for power not unlike those of their industrial rivals, the owners and managers. Perhaps the most revealing feature of news photographs, depicting labor leaders on one side of a consulting table and managers on the other, is that the reader has to be told which side is which; all look remarkably alike.

The Christian estimate likewise saves us from gullibility about education. Undoubtedly we need schools and may rejoice whenever any young person is given a chance to learn, but education is no panacea, for the reason that those whose business is the conduct of schools and colleges have their own human temptations to which they frequently succumb. It is an open secret that many college faculties are scenes of ill-disguised hatreds of a particularly bitter variety. The same is sometimes true of church leadership and the disgrace of many churches is the lack of love within them. The quality of the buildings and the impressiveness of the hierarchy does not seem to mitigate the problem. The sad truth is that all of us are lineal descendants of Noah.

Though the advance security against false and delusive hopes is itself a great gain, which this emphasis in Christian thinking provides, another and even more beneficent result is the way in which the realistic emphasis actually helps us to do better. The doctrine of indigenous sin is beneficent in practice because it saves us from the angelic fallacy and encourages us to do something positive to overcome some of the worst features of our situations. The Christian realization of man as a sinner helped the founding fathers of our nation to avoid the optimistic deductions to which they were tempted by French ideas and led them to institute the system of checks and balances which is so prominent a feature of our Constitution. Our system makes it extremely difficult for a lover of power to take full advantage of the situation. This beneficent result arises from the recognition that no man is wholly trustworthy, not even the patriot leader or reformer. The totalitarian system, so eloquently expounded by Mussolini in his days of personal glory, was based on the principle that the average citizen cannot be trusted with the vote. This skeptical principle was a partial but distorted application of the Christian realism. If he had applied this realism more fully and more consistently, Mussolini would have seen that it likewise means that the leader cannot himself be given a wholly free hand, for he, too, is in the human situation and can be corrupted by power. Reinhold Niebuhr's fortunate expression in his lectures at Stanford

University applies directly at this point.[3] Democracy, he has told us, is made necessary by the fact that man is a sinner. It is made possible by the fact that he knows it.

This fundamental insight shows us why we need the Church and its ministrations. Men may be virtuous without the Church, at least for a generation, but the time comes when the notion that we are naturally good becomes patently false. If we *were* angels we should not need the help of prayer and public worship, but far from being angels we are very feeble reeds. The man who thinks he can do very well in his own power is actually simple-minded and not very penetrating in his understanding of human life in general or his own situation in particular. The Christian doctrine of indigenous sin may dim some of our romantic hopes about what human life may become, but, in the end, it is wonderfully helpful because it gives us a rational basis for concrete effort in avoiding in advance some of the worst failures of ourselves and others. It saves us from all the false optimism of naturalism which, when it goes sour, often becomes the dangerous cynicism on which totalitarian systems thrive.

Valuable as is the current emphasis on indigenous sin at the middle of our century, an emphasis which transcends all party lines, it *can be* dangerous. The danger is the common one of drawing negative conclusions from positive premises. The positive premise that man does whatever he does as a sinner is obviously true, but it is illicit to draw from this the negative conclusion that men, anywhere, are wholly removed from the divine love and

[3] *The Children of Light and the Children of Darkness.*

influence. Though man is a sinner he is also a child of God, made in God's image, for whom the Father yearns and in whom God has placed a witness, even when it is not heeded. If the doctrine of man as sinner is presented as the *whole truth* about man it becomes a distortion and therefore a heresy. The truth is that no man is righteous, and this we need to know, but the gospel is that God reaches out to every man and this we need to know far more vividly.

The second major emphasis of the theology of the past quarter century is that upon the uniqueness of the events to which the Christian faith points men and women in this or any other time. Just as the first emphasis is a strong reaction against the liberal estimate of man's inherent goodness, the second is an equally strong reaction against the liberal tendency to think of religion as a set of ideas about God which are universal in the sense that they are independent of particular times and particular places. In many academic centers, in the past, and in some contemporary ones not in step with the modern mood, the Christian religion has been presented as just one religion among others, while all religion is presented as "man's search for the good life" or "man's search for God." In this older intellectual setting popular courses were those in comparative religions or in that form of the philosophy of religion which made very sure that no more emphasis would be given to events in Palestine than to contemplations under the Bo tree.

The older thinking that was academically respectable was often concerned with natural religion rather than with revealed religion. A symptom of this is seen in the famous Gifford Lectures, the most distinguished series in the modern world, which are supposedly devoted entirely to those arguments about God and immortality to which a man may arrive by his own unaided reason. Karl Barth was able to lecture on the basis of the Gifford Trust only by a frankly stated rejection of the intellectual basis of that Trust.

There have always been millions of humble Christians, particularly those called Fundamentalists, who have rejected this emphasis on natural religion and have stressed unique revelation, but the important feature of the new development is that such an emphasis is now made by the intellectuals. The modern Christian thinkers of many different traditions tend to reject completely the notion that the Christian religion is just one religion among the other religions of the world. One of the clearest and most persuasive statements of the conclusion that the Christian faith is tied up for better or for worse, with unique events in unique places, is found in the Hulsean Lectures of Professor H. G. Wood, delivered at the University of Cambridge under the title "Christianity and the Nature of History."

It is somewhat shocking, to some, to realize for the first time that the Biblical record is far more concerned with events than it is with ideas. Ideas there are, but they are subordinated to events. The conviction, usually unstated, is that God reveals Himself much more fully in history than in nature or in any other way. There are a few references to nature, in the Bible, intended to suggest a natural revelation, but they are exceptions. In Amos we are told to seek Him who made the Pleiades and Orion, while Psalm 19 says that the heavens declare the glory of God, but there are not many more such passages. Where there is one such passage referring to nature there are scores referring to history. The Hebrews and early Christians did not invent the philosophy of religion; that was done by the Greeks. It is not the Bible, but the tenth book of Plato's *Laws* that gives the best early formulation of the cosmological and teleological arguments.

The men who wrote the words of the Bible were contented, for the most part, with telling a story. When Stephen and Paul were asked to justify their faith they gave the record and let it rest. He brought us out of Egypt against dreadful odds; He took us through the wilderness when we could not help ourselves; He carried us into the promised land; He brought forth a Savior, who lived, died and rose again. The revelation, they held, was in what had *occurred* and never primarily in doctrines or notions. The occurrences were wonderfully and, from some philosophical viewpoints, scandalously particularized. They came at particular times in particular places and had about them a once-for-allness. Christianity, therefore, is not merely a set of moral and spiritual teachings, not a theory about life, not a speculation, but a reaction to a series of alleged facts. The upshot is that Christian history is vastly more important than is Christian theory. The heart of the gospel is the exciting historical fact that the eternal Word became flesh and dwelt among men. All history for all men, Buddhists, Jews, Mohammedans and all others, cen-

ters, if only they knew it, on the incarnation, crucifixion
and resurrection. The Apostle's Creed is largely an asser-
tion that certain events occurred, not in some supersensual
sphere, but under Pontius Pilate.

One aspect of this emphasis on unique events is that
the characteristic interpreters and intellectual defenders
of the Christian faith are now far less apologetic than they
formerly were. Once in recent times, the faith seemed so
shaky that numerous Christians became very excited when
some famous scientist was willing to affirm his belief in
God. The indecent haste to exploit such news was a symptom of profound uncertainty and insecurity on the part
of the supposedly faithful. It was almost as though the
scientist had done God an honor by his gracious willingness to believe in Him. Ministers, for a while, quoted
Eddington and Jeans along with the Bible.[4] The degree
to which this is changed is well shown by the relatively
small ripple made among Christian thinkers, by the books
of the late Lecomte du Noüy.

Nearly every strong and beneficent intellectual tendency
carries with it its own dangers and the emphasis on unique
revelation is no exception to this rule. A position becomes
a heresy when, though true, it is stressed so strongly that it
becomes separated from the main body of truth. Some of
the continental theologians have thus been guilty of making a heresy out of the doctrine of Christ. They do this by
an almost complete failure to mention either God as
Creator or the Holy Spirit as Comforter. In their effort to

[4] The whole of Eddington's Swarthmore Lecture, in 1929, was sent across
the Atlantic by cable.

stress the one great historical revelation they even mini-
mize the work of the Living Christ in the human heart
today. The heresy of these Christians may be called "Unitarianism of the Second Person." The old-fashioned Bos-
tonian Unitarianism was that of the First Person, while
the Pentecostal sects tend to produce a Unitarianism of
the Third Person, but the lesson of Christian history
seems to be that the fullest truth lies in the rejection of
even Second Person Unitarianism and in the espousal of
a full-bodied Trinitarian faith.

As we approach the middle of the century we are beginning to have several acute criticisms of the emphasis on
unique revelation on the part of thinkers who appreciate
the gains that have been made in theological vigor in our
troubled times, but who are keenly aware of the error
which creeps in when the position becomes extreme. Thus
we are feeling the criticism that too much of this theology
has suffered by espousing the irrational. Complete irration-
ality has no defense against the demonic or the perverted. If
faith is essentially irrational, how do we know which faith
to espouse? Why not follow Hitler or some new cult leader
rather than Christ? Anyone who attempts to answer this
question is forced to begin to discuss *credentials,* but we
cannot discuss credentials without employing reason. Sheer
faith is sheer nonsense, and if we leave out teachings or
moral results, there is no essential difference between the
word "Christ" and any other word.[5]

[5] For a trenchant criticism of the irrationalism inherent in some theology
of the recent past see L. Harold DeWolf, *The Religious Revolt against
Reason* (New York: Harper & Brothers, 1949).

Much as the continental theologians have stressed the centrality of Christ in history, they have often shown a curious hesitancy to pay much attention to the recorded sayings of this same Person. For some strange reason it seems to them easier to stress the Word than the words. We can be grateful to Dean Sperry for his timely criticism at this point.

The truth of the matter seems to be that thinkers of this type feel no sense of religious debt or theological obligation to the recorded words of Jesus. His ministry and His sayings apparently lie to one side of the mark as far as the Christian religion is concerned. There are, it is true, in these books, occasional citations from *John,* and more frequent quotations from the Epistles. As far as one can make out, the only important truths for our religion to be found in the Gospels—apart from the affirmation that the kingdom is at hand—are the prologue to John and the account of the crucifixion and resurrection. The historical necessity of the crucifixion is conceded as being an integral part of the divine plan. No attention whatsoever is paid to the ecclesiastical and political causes for the death of Jesus.[6]

The third emphasis of the new theology is on what may usefully be termed the Total Gospel. In the childhood of those now in middle life our Christian faith was assumed as a decent and wholly natural phase of our national existence, but seldom was that faith presented as the necessary price of survival. Faith was sometimes presented as an absolute necessity for the life everlasting, but it was not presented as an absolute necessity for the total structure

[6] Willard L. Sperry, *Jesus Then and Now* (New York: Harper & Brothers, 1949) , pp. 199, 200.

of human life on this globe. The philosophy of civilization
and its bearing on the relevance of the gospel was not at
all a common theme.[7]

So greatly is the mood now changed, and the message
changed with it, that such a phrase as "the race with
catastrophe" is on many lips and is certain to be heard in
pulpits in every part of the land. The late Professor
Berdyaev and many others have seen to that. The new
preaching has been marked, accordingly, by a recovery of
the sense of urgency that has sometimes brought a wholly
new vigor into the message. The faith is presented, not
as adornment, but as a terrible necessity if man's deep
sickness is to be cured before it is too late. For all such
preaching the golden text is "Work while it is day, for
the night cometh when no man can work."

Once a great deal of preaching consisted of attractively
written essays, sometimes about the nature of goodness,
sometimes about the beauties of nature. It was pointed out
that flowers grew in the spring and that children's faces
were fresh and lovely. Along with such preaching went
interesting and informing book reviews, sometimes as
appropriate to the meeting of the women's club as to the
hour of worship.

We can hardly overstate the degree to which such preaching is now dated; it is almost nonexistent in the contemporary pulpit. The characteristic preaching now is far

[7] The whole subject of civilization is now central to advanced religious
thinking. Two famous theologians, Herbert G. Wood of England and
Emil Brunner of Switzerland, have published volumes with the identical
title, *Christianity and Civilization,* while Arnold Toynbee has published
a lecture by the same title.

more masculine and is more truly represented by Paul Tillich's volume, *The Shaking of the Foundations.* The new preaching is a modern surrogate of the older preaching of damnation and salvation, for there is a damnation that has been vividly illustrated and what we seek is a desperate remedy. In this recovery of urgency the Bible again makes sense to thoughtful readers. Once its language seemed overdrawn, but that is true no longer. It seems again to be a contemporary book because it is about refugees and dictatorships and colossal deceptions and wanton cruelty and urgent words. Once it was hard to understand Christ's words as he sent out the seventy disciples, for he told them to hurry, to avoid excess baggage and not to linger when people did not listen. His words were meaningless except in the context of crisis, but now we, for a generation, have lived in the mood of crisis. It is not so much that the Bible is a commentary on current history as that current history is a commentary on the Bible, making much of its ancient meaning suddenly clear.

Once we saw a great contrast between the individual gospel and the social gospel and these alternatives produced something of a cleavage in the Christian movement. The individual gospel dealt with the way an individual person could save his soul from hell, while the social gospel dealt with the application of the teachings of Jesus to such problems as poverty, war, race prejudice, and industrial strife. Now, happily, we have come into a time when this dichotomy has been largely transcended. What we see now is that the predicament is that of all mankind, including both our individual and social destinies. The sickness is a total sickness and the gospel must therefore be a total gospel. If individual salvation was the thesis and social salvation the antithesis, then total salvation is the synthesis.

The burden of the total message of the total gospel is that we shall die—*unless!* We have been impressed anew with the doleful record of societies which have ceased to be. They could not sustain themselves, even though they developed agriculture, art and technology, because they lacked the extra that could keep these potential benefits from becoming a curse.[8] The story of Sodom and Gomorrah is perennial.

The most persuasive presentation of the total gospel in our time has come by taking the offensive against paganism. It is a poor and thankless business to stand back and defend religion, but men may listen if we carry the war into the camp of the enemy and show, in detail, how it is that paganism is fundamentally parasitical and self defeating. Paganism can exhibit, for a while, some of the borrowed fruits of Christian culture, but it cannot keep them alive, even for its own sake. A mere power culture is bound to fall eventually by its own weight, partly because it cannot provide a favorable climate for the growth of science on which its very power depends. In the same way we can keep the offensive and show not only the impotence of mere ethics, but also the insufficiency of individual religion, separated from the sustaining and worshiping community which is the church.

There is a subtle danger in this virile attack in that,

8 This seems to be the meaning of the story of the sons of Lamech. Cf. Genesis 4:19-24.

unless we are superbly careful, we shall seem to make the gospel merely instrumental. We run the risk of seeming to say: Let us revive our religion because thereby we can save our culture.[9] This would indicate that the culture is more important than the faith which sustains it, since the means is naturally inferior in value to the end which it serves. Sometimes this mistake is actually made, as when people are encouraged to be devout in order to save thereby our capitalist order.

The way to avoid this real and serious danger is to make it clear to ourselves and to others that what we seek to save is not a culture, but *men*. It is men and women who are precious and it is men and women for whom Christ died. It is men whom God made in His own image and whom God loves, no matter how sinful they are. The gospel is made for men and if it is people about whom we are concerned, rather than some system of our making, we get the elements in the right order of priority. It is man who is sick and who needs a physician; the total gospel is the remedy.

Here, then, are three marks of the new virile theology of our time and together they form a consistent whole of remarkable power. This composite is not the only theological emphasis of our time, but it is the one which has the most intellectual and moral vigor and the most hope of making a difference in human destiny. The emergence

[9] Even the titles of some of our better books suggest, if we are not careful, this instrumental relation. A case in point is *Can Christianity Save Civilization?* by Walter M. Horton, and *Does Civilization Need Religion?* by Reinhold Niebuhr. Both authors reject the notion of the gospel as instrumental, however.

of this composite teaching is one of the evidences that ours is really a time of new reformation when life again breaks through the crust.

Living as we do at the middle of the century, when these vigorous emphases have already been made and partly understood, we are in a peculiarly fortunate position. We should be able to take advantage of this virile theology without falling into the errors which have finally become conspicuous. We should be able to profit by the realistic emphasis or man's sinful nature without falling into the particular errors of neo-orthodoxy and we ought to be able to respond to the wonder of objective revelation without denying the place of reason or the trustworthiness of religious experience. In short, ours is a fortunate time in theology because the ground is prepared for a true catholicity. Fortunately, the main lines of this have already been shown by some who have stood above the battle cries of partisan emphasis. Perhaps the finest lead of all was that given by William Temple when he wrote his famous Gifford Lectures, *Nature, Man and God*. In this magnificent book we see twentieth-century theology at its maturest and best. It constitutes one of the strongest evidences of light in darkness.

CHAPTER IV

The Emergence of Lay Religion

I hazard the prophecy that that religion will conquer which can render clear to popular understanding some eternal greatness incarnate in the passage of temporal fact.

ALFRED NORTH WHITEHEAD

EXCITING as the new theology is and wonderful as it is to live in a day when the intellectual buttresses of our faith are so strong, there is something that is still more exciting, the springing up of lay religion in so many spots. We are living in one of the times when a development seems to come spontaneously and independently at many points at once. Lay religion is one of the chief marks of the Christian Renaissance in Japan, but it is appearing likewise in Europe and America. It appears in both Catholic and Protestant circles, the Catholic movement of greatest hope in this regard being the Christopher movement and the Protestant development being a vigorous reassertion and new appreciation of the thrilling Protestant principle of the priesthood of the believer.

Everywhere the movement is based on the recognition that the crisis is too serious to be met by the clergy alone. The task is so great that it cannot be met unless it is faced

76

resolutely by the common efforts of all the members at once. This means, necessarily, a noticeable dimming of the distinction between clergy and laity and in some areas it leads, gloriously, to the acceptance of the early Christian ideal of the complete abolition of the laity—with all Christians as recruits in a common cause. Many have begun for the first time in their lives to ask seriously what it means to be a minister. Is a minister one who is called by the title "Reverend" or is he one who serves as "Christ's man" whatever his means of making a living? Is a minister, some are bold enough to ask, one who has been "ordained," who has had some words said over him, or is he simply one who ministers?

We understand this new phase of Christian history better if we contrast it with the phase which it is beginning to displace. It is the sorrowful truth that a great deal of our religion in the recent past has been, for the most part, clergyman's religion. This has been true of both Catholics and Protestants, in spite of the Reformation emphasis that should have made a permanent difference. Our presuppositions in this matter are shown by our current speech. In the past, if it was said of a man that he was entering the Church, it was often supposed that this meant that he was entering the priesthood or the ministry. If a young man became deeply concerned about the conduct of the Christian cause his neighbors would ask him if he were a ministerial student. Now, fortunately, this is already beginning to change. Now, in some up-to-date circles it is wholly possible to understand a doctor who is an unapologetic and committed Christian without the supposition that he is preparing to go abroad as a medical missionary. Instead, it may be realized by some that he is simply a thoughtful man who has begun to understand how close to the abyss we are moving and who desires, consequently, to put the main energies of his life into the main struggle of the human race at this juncture. The change is a change for the better.

Great as are the names of the men who are producing contemporary theology, and moving as their central ideas become when they impinge on sensitive minds, these men have the handicap of being professionals. There are many who will not listen to professionals for the very reason that these thinkers *are* professionals. Whatever they say or do is minimized in advance by the potential listeners who pay little attention to what such men say because they are expected to say good things; that is their job. Anticlericalism is not always vocal or self-conscious in the world, but it has gone very deep and is part of the unconscious mood of millions. If there is some truly healing movement in our time it will have to be a movement which avoids the onus of clericalism and seems close to the life of ordinary people.

It must be said, in honesty, that a great part of what is most precious in our Christian society has, all along, been lay religion. Sometimes our very familiarity with the Sunday-school movement has kept up from realizing how radically new it was when it began and what a burst of life it constituted. Recently a Protestant minister, when visiting Europe, casually remarked that in the church which he served there was a Bible school which met every Sunday morning at nine-thirty and that it was taught by fifty-six trained lay teachers. The European listeners would hardly believe what he said. To some of them it was unthinkable. How could most of the sacred teaching be in the hands of amateurs, and how could there be so many who were willing? Many of us have seen this all our lives without realizing how wonderful it has been.

The Adult School Movement in England had a remarkable effect in an earlier generation. What it often meant was that a lay form of Christianity existed side by side with a clerical form and with almost no sense of competition. Something similar to this has occurred in Norway for many years. All over the world the Young Men's Christian Association and its sister organization have been active for evangelistic purposes, but they have had lay leadership. John R. Mott, the most honored single sponsor of the ecumenical movement, has looked upon himself all his life as a layman. The Disciples of Christ, who celebrate Holy Communion every Sunday in all their local churches, have long shown their fundamentally democratic character by the presence of laymen in the chancel on this devout occasion. One layman prays before the distribution of the loaf and the other prays before the distribution of the cup. They stand on a level with the minister. For three hundred years the Society of Friends has carried on its far-flung work in many lands without the assistance of an ordained or a separated clergy.

What we see now is the emergence of several such movements all at once. A vigorous illustration of what is occurring is provided by the experience of the new Ecumenical Institute at Bossy, Switzerland, near the shores of Lake

Geneva. This new venture, made possible by the gift of John D. Rockefeller, Jr., is devoted to the study of theology, yet those for whose sake the theology is taught are not professionally religious, but instead are persons whose daily lives are concerned with the common pursuits of common life. The students are mature laymen and lay women who, after their brief but intensive studies, go back to their jobs as housewives, physicians, business people or teachers, but they go with new insight into the ways in which their common jobs can facilitate the growth and application of the gospel. Already the influence of this center is being strongly felt in many parts of Europe.

Another lay movement of considerable promise is the Christian Frontier Movement of England, of which Mrs. Kathleen Bliss is secretary. The whole idea of the Frontier is the conduct of the Christian campaign by means of common professions and common work. The central council of the Christian Frontier Movement is made up of lay persons, each of whom is representative of one of the great secular ways of earning a living or performing human service. So valuable has this approach become that we may expect some religious conferences in the future to organize their discussions chiefly along vocational lines and thus come closer to common life. Instead of organizing a conference in long standardized ways, dividing into sections devoted to problems, we could organize it on the basis of work, the various vocations struggling to find their particular way of promoting the common cause.

In America there are many new evidences of lay evangelism, some appearing in the various denominations and others cutting across denominational lines. One of the most effective of the latter is the Laymen's Movement for a Christian World, which attracts much interest by its annual conference in New York and which has helped numerous men to find new life in that they become lay evangelists, though they continue to earn their livings in what are called secular professions and businesses. One inspired by this movement may earn his living as a publisher, but he may come to look upon his publishing primarily as a ministry, a way in which he can influence our present civilization by helping to determine what people read. Similarly a doctor, particularly one devoted to mental health, may be a strong influence in medical circles, guiding his fellow physicians to the place where they will be willing to make fuller use of the immense resources for health which are involved in the faith of Christ.

The Christopher Movement, founded by Father James Keller, is an attempt within the framework of Roman Catholicism, to encourage the religious activity of all believers, each in his own secular job. It is central to the Christopher or "Christ-bearer" idea that God has put a "little bit of the missionary" in every human being. Men really love to be missionaries, but they can be missionaries without going abroad and without entering the priesthood. The Christopher idea, says the founder, "merely applies to the heart of America the same simple approach used by a missioner in bringing Christ into a pagan city in China."[1]

1 James Keller, *You Can Change the World* (New York: Longmans, Green and Company, 1949), p. 320.

In Washington, D. C., are Breakfast Clubs made up especially of senators and congressmen who breakfast weekly in the Capitol and who seek to face their political responsibilities on their knees. These men are a small minority and it is well known that for one such gathering there are scores of cocktail parties, but in the long run the kind of life which goes on when men seek to learn what it means to be Christian politicians may be more formative of the future than we are likely to suppose.

That Japan is having a new burst of religious life with a rapid increase in the Christian populations is well known, but what is not so well known is the fact that much of this is a lay movement. In the United Church of Japan the public worship is as often the scene of vocal prayers by lay members as by clergymen and those who thus participate are often women. This represents real novelty in the life of the Far East, but is coming as an outgrowth or symptom of the new spiritual vigor. Though America has long sent missionaries to Japan it is possible that America may learn from the practice of those who have been the objects of our missionary zeal, as well as our hated enemies in war.

An interesting new approach to national regeneration is seen in Greece, especially in the vitality of lay activities in a country that has often been priest-ridden. The most hopeful development in Greece is that of the Zoé Movement, which, instead of drawing Greeks away from the traditional Orthodox Church, is trying to revive the Church from within. A religious press is published, chiefly by laymen, and is so successful that American visitors report it is more widely read than is the secular press. Laymen are printing sermons in order to stir up better preaching among the clergy! They have established many Sunday schools. Movements of slightly different nature, but with marked vitality, are making a difference in both Finland and Hungary. In both France and Holland ventures have been made in the publication of Christian newspapers.

Perhaps the most exciting new development in this general direction is the recent suggestion to the Foreign Missionary Conference of America to engage in a foreign missionary procedure radically different from most of those known before. The noble missionary enterprise of the last one hundred fifty years has been carried on, for the most part, by persons sent abroad by boards and paid by them through funds given generously by the local home churches. Now the vision is that the Christian cause abroad can be immensely expanded by training able people in secular activities and offering them to business or governmental agencies. If we can send a deeply committed Christian to China as an employee of Standard Oil, that is as good an undertaking as sending him under the Presbyterian Board. Perhaps it is even better, because the Standard Oil man does not have to overcome the onus of being a professional who may be accused of saying what he says because he has a stake in it.

If a foreign government needs technicians, why should we not send technicians who are at the same time unapologetically devout and who will begin at once to work on the moral as well as the technological level. If a backward country needs teachers, paid for by the government,

who can attack the problem of illiteracy, there is no reason
why they should not have some of the people whom Frank
Laubach has trained in his remarkably successful method.
If we begin to understand the true wonder of this approach to the problem of world regeneration we may develop in some places a new kind of education, specifically
aimed at the training of men and women who can be lay
missionaries of this new type. After they are trained and
we are sure of both their competence and their commitment, we can approach the agencies which need help and
nominate these persons for the positions that wait to be
filled.

At home great strides are being made in the program of
visitation evangelism, a program in which the major effort
in calling upon new people for enlistment in the Christian cause is done by laymen, working in teams. The ministers, in most instances, are the ones who train the laymen
in the right ways to conduct such campaigns and frequently
the method succeeds, not only because it increases so
greatly the number of actual visits, but also because some
lay people respond more warmly to the calls of other laymen than to the calls of clergymen. In America, alone, over
one million men and women have now been trained in
this kind of evangelistic approach.

All this is very exciting because the emergence of lay
religion has often been, in the past, one of the first evidences of new vigor. Religion can survive for centuries, as
a clergyman's or a priest's religion though it survives in a
dull state, but when it really thrives it always bursts such
bonds. The first of the writing prophets of ancient Israel,

and thus the originator of a cumulative tradition that has influenced the whole of Western civilization, was in no sense a priest. Amos said he was not even a prophet or the son of a prophet. He was a simple layman, a herdsman and a gatherer of sycamore fruit, but he heard the Lord's message and had to deliver it. His ministry was not that of status, but rather that of urgency and power.

We must never allow ourselves to forget that the Christian religion itself likewise began as a lay movement. Among the twelve whom Christ chose to receive his most intimate teaching and to carry on his message, not one was a priest, bishop or rabbi. Not one was professionally religious in any sense. Some were fishermen and one, at least, was a publican. We might go farther and say truly that the early Christian movement was essentially anticlerical. Those whom Christ denounced most fiercely were not publicans or harlots, but scribes and pharisees. In fact, he was very tender with the unrespectable sinners, but he was fiercely denunciatory of the conventional upholders of pious respectability. He went so far as to say, "Call no man Father, for one is your Father." How those who claim to be Christians and use the term "Father" as a religious appellation get around this is a continuing mystery. But Christ also said, "Be not called Rabbi, Rabbi." This does not disturb us until we realize that probably the best modern translation of Rabbi is "Doctor" or "Reverend." When we see how thousands of clergymen are called doctor, irrespective of degrees, we understand a little of what Jesus must have meant when he intimated that it would be very easy to call him "Lord, Lord" and yet not do the things that he said. Why is it that religious gatherings are often marked by a greater punctiliousness about the use of honorific titles than are those of people who make no claim to be Christian at all?

Christ gave the kind of message that is wholly incompatible with the very notion of a hierarchy. He agreed that in the secular world, that is, among the Gentiles, men sought for power and prestige, but he was trying, he said, to set up an order, diametrically opposed to this. It follows that the very idea of a "Prince of the Church" is an unchristian idea.

In spite of the revolutionary teaching of Christ the crust of ecclesiasticism slowly forms in various generations and then must be burst open from beneath by a new lay religion. The sorrow is that the new life in time becomes crystallized, as occurred earlier in the Franciscan Movement, and more recently in the Salvation Army, so that finally it, too, is part of the crust that must be broken by some new thrust. Our job now is to facilitate a contemporary break-through and it ought to be said that countless concerned clergymen welcome this with all their hearts. They are by no means satisfied with their present situations and they agree heartily with Emil Brunner that a clergyman's religion is always a heresy.

The good minister is not one who desires to be the whole show or the center of attention. He desires rather to be a catalytic agent, stirring up lay members to activity and perfectly satisfied if his contribution is not seen or known. The best minister makes himself progressively unnecessary. Nearly every good minister will agree that the Christian ideal is that of a body of believers all of whom are participators in the evangelistic enterprise, but many men are handicapped by convention and are looking for help in the enterprise of beginning to put into effect reforms that they know ought to occur.

Today some Methodist ministers are recruiting able laymen so that a different one may preach each month on the great essentials of the faith. Colleges are sometimes using some of their own students in witness to their faith and find that the public meetings in which this occurs are often more effective than are those addressed by some able men from the outside. Some ministers are beginning to be theological professors in their own communities, using a technique not unlike that perfected by the Great Book Movement. Some ministers who have been expected to offer prayer at public occasions are wisely refusing to do so, because they know that they, when they do it, are depriving some layman of experience in the very kind of expression of devotion that may make for his spiritual growth.

All of us may be greatly helped by a new clarification of what a church really is or ought to be. A Christian society is not like an ancient pagan cult in which worshipers go one by one to some shrine, which for some superstitious reason is called a holy place. We see some of this in the modern world, but we ought to be on our guard against it, for it is sub-Christian. The dried-up arm of an alleged saint, such as was recently publicized in the popular press, has nothing whatever to do with real Christianity. It is a good thing for puzzled and needy people to have quiet places to which they can retire from the streets for meditation and prayer, but it is not a good thing to encourage them in the pagan notion that there is some magical significance in particular holy objects or holy places. The New Testament is quite specific on this. "The Lord of heaven and earth," we are told, "dwells not in temples made with hands."[2] Vital religion is never concerned with dead men's bones.

A Christian society, moreover, is not a collection of people who at regular or irregular intervals sit as spectators while a minister preaches to them or entertains them, and then go home with the feeling that their Christian task is accomplished for the week. Those whose religion consists in this gesture of respectability are perhaps better than idolaters, but not much better. Instead of this, a Christian church is a Society of Witnesses. Note that Christ, immediately after he had called the infant church the salt of the earth, went on to say that members must let their lights shine before men. He left them as a band of persons whose lives had been so much enkindled by his own, that the spread of light was their central vocation. He left behind an order of lay evangelists and the essence of their fellowship was their function. They existed for only one primary purpose—*to evangelize*.

If we should grasp the New Testament conception of the Church, lay religion, including a large amount of lay preaching, would be universally expected and encouraged. What is happening in the Christian Movement in the middle of our century of the civil war is that we are beginning to grasp this conception. Our fundamental insight is that

2 Acts 17:24.

the main job of the Church is not to enjoy itself or bask in its own goodness, but to evangelize, and this necessitates lay religion by consequence, inasmuch as the job is manifestly too large to be accomplished by the ministers working alone. Once this logical deduction is made we are faced with the task of thinking up new and creative ways by which the outreach of millions of laymen can be made. If this is ably done and if it catches on generally, the resultant change in the total Christian program will reach an entirely different level, since the advance will be by multiplication rather than addition.

Up to now we have tended, for the most part, to think of the spread of the Christian Way and adherence to the Christian Cause as coming about chiefly through the instrumentality of the Sunday morning or Sunday evening sermon. The lay people help, of course, by ushering, by looking after the physical setting, by providing money, by prayer and by mere attendance. These efforts, in countless local congregations, now constitute the high point of the week, the climactic event to which all else points. The sermon is a kind of omega. The lay members are exhorted to live better through the coming week and they are undoubtedly strengthened for both their tasks and their sorrows, but seldom are they sent out as genuine ambassadors.

There is an alternative to this conventional conception. This alternative is centered in the idea that the service on Sunday morning is more like a beginning than an end. The members of the Witness Society gather together on the Lord's Day and one of their number, because he is gifted as a stirrer up of hearts and a wise counselor, briefs his fellow workers and helps to begin a new week in their ministry. They will share in the world's labor, selling vacuum cleaners or counting money or disciplining little children, but always the real priority will be given to the fact that they are volunteers in a Christian army who have accepted the Lordship of Christ. The job is too big to be done in one day a week; it takes all seven.

Humble Christians who accept this alternative of what a church ought to be and *may* be will not be satisfied with conventional approaches to men and women. Certainly they will not wait at the Church for people to come to hear them. The trouble with that procedure is not that we are unwilling to feed the sheep, but that the wrong sheep show up at the feeding place. An imaginative and aroused Christian layman might, for instance, undergo the necessary discipline to prepare himself to write a successful Broadway play that would shake complacent men as they ought to be shaken. Whoever writes the plays touches the people where they *are*. One of the popular Broadway productions cannot promise a seat in less than four months, but there do not seem to be many churches which are in that predicament.

The play *The Death of a Salesman* is a great play and deserves its awards, but it has often been noted that its main effect is negative. It shows the relentless action of the moral law, but there is no redemption in it. Now the contention is that there *could* be redemption in such a play and it would not necessarily, for that reason, be sentimental or obviously pious. Men are moved by the vision of greatness, and redemption can be great. It may be necessary to add, at this point, that this suggestion has nothing whatever in common with the effort, sometimes made in the motion pictures, to use the entertainment business to enhance the power or popularity of a particular denomination or institution. That is not the idea at all. A play could be deeply and profoundly religious, but as undenominational as the plays of Shakespeare.

Another possible outlet of lay religion is in the general field of writing, especially writing for books and for the secular magazines. The writer can write from the Christian point of view, whatever the subject, and he can make all his writing a ministry. Success in this entails a great deal of hard work, as does any worth-while endeavor, but many who are now unproductive could school themselves for this work if they would. It is not enough to write; we must write so that our words will be read by the people we hope to reach. To this end we must use imagination in regard to the size of books, in regard to titles and in regard to style. The example of C. S. Lewis is highly admirable in all this. He has trained himself to say religious things in such a way that thousands will read his words, though they would never think, at the time, of attending a church or of listening to an ordinary religious discourse. It is obvious that Lewis has done no more than touch the fringes of this field, and we need many more in all countries to engage in such disciplined and intelligent evangelism. It must be remembered that it is effective precisely in so far as it is disciplined and intelligent.

The rule in all this lay religion of our time is the principle that if the mountain won't come to Mohammed, then

Mohammed will go to the mountain. If the people don't come to church, and often it is not surprising that they do not, Christians must go to them wherever they are. If we are to walk with most men we must start walking where they already are, and not wait for them to come to us. If they read *The Reader's Digest* rather than *The Christian Century,* Christians must try to write for the *Digest.* If they are in places of entertainment, Christians must go there. Some might not approve, but we have the example of the Lord on our side. The accusation of the respectable gossips was that he was a winebibber and a friend of harlots. If people are in the labor union, meet them there and finally they may listen, especially if those who speak are members for the good reason that they are common toilers also. If men are at the Kiwanis Club luncheon rather than at the prayer meeting, then the luncheon may be a good place to operate.

If we are discouraged at the patent difficulty of breaking out of the familiar ruts and starting new approaches to human need we may be heartened by the successful experience of the Gideons. Almost all modern Americans are aware of the existence of Bibles in hotels all over the land, but many do not know how they got there. There are some, no doubt, who consider the ubiquity of the Gideon Bibles amusing, but the judgment of such persons is not very important and the evidence shows that great numbers have been brought to the knowledge of God by this simple means.

The Gideons were formed just fifty years ago and, like most creative movements, began in the minds of a few modest men. Two traveling men shared evening devotions in a Wisconsin hotel and found the experience so helpful that they determined later to form an Association of Christian Travelling Men. The name Gideons was chosen because of the story found in the seventh chapter of Judges. It was another way of saying that they looked upon themselves as a commando group, small but maneuverable and hard hitting. The growth of the movement in a bare half century has been phenomenal. There were only three members when they organized in July, 1899, but the society has now placed more than two and a quarter million Bibles in hotels and other institutions. During World War II this voluntary society distributed over nine million Testaments with Psalms to the men and women of the armed forces. At their recent fiftieth anniversary gathering in Milwaukee it was reported that they have now given away to American school children four million volumes similar to those distributed to the armed forces, but with Proverbs added. What the Gideons really do is to give some idea of what may be accomplished by those who combine imagination with zeal, trying to reach people where they are instead of lamenting that they are not elsewhere. There must be other contributions waiting to be done that would be quite as concrete and quite as striking as the unique contribution made by the Gideons. Not all the inventions are in technology.

Some people are naturally critical of what seems to be the dominant and somewhat narrow theology characteristic of the Gideons, but it ought to be remembered that what is unique about them is not this particular theo-

logical emphasis. Many millions have shared this theology
without the brilliance of attack which the Gideons have
demonstrated, and it is their brilliance of attack on the
problem that must be emulated. We must say for them,
furthermore, that they have done very little to impress a
particular theological interpretation upon potential readers, but have, with great wisdom, let the Bible speak for
itself. They are in great and heartening contrast, in this
regard, to those who have put out Bibles which have so
insinuated the interpretative notes into the reader's mind
that the unwary cannot differentiate, in subsequent
thought, between the notes and the text.[3]

An increasing proportion of the new Christian campaign for a redeemed world may consist of the formation
of new orders devoted to the vocational implications of
the gospel, doing for other occupations what the Gideon
Society has done for commercial travelers. These will be
Christian vocational guilds, each with its appropriate discipline and minimum organization. There is great promise
in the idea of a guild of Christian statesmen, who undertake the rigors and the temptations of political life with
the idea of thereby making their most effective witness.
The beginnings of this are already made, but the development is more advanced in the formation of guilds of Christian scholars or Christian professors. These men and
women, who may teach any secular subject, are committed
to teaching as a Christian vocation. They are wise enough

[3] An illustration of this is the Schofield Reference Bible which has had
a much more potent influence on the Christian movement in America than
is generally recognized. It is dangerous partly because it is well done.

to know that they will often be lonely or even ridiculed in those academic settings in which naturalism is a rigid orthodoxy, but they propose to go into our great pagan universities as missionaries. Knowing in advance that they are missionaries is a great help, since it helps men to avoid initial surprises and disappointments.

Great strides might be made soon in the formation of a guild of Christian doctors or of nurses. The majority of practicing physicians are outside the active work of any church and the very nature of their profession makes regular attendance at public worship impossible for many, but some physicians are very active in the men's work of the churches. They may be restive under the steady preaching of professionals, but they might do wonders if sufficiently encouraged to engage in their own amateur efforts. Another important group of men that is now ripe for the guild idea are the atomic scientists. Their first flush of moral enthusiasm is over, but many of them continue to show themselves to be as morally sensitive as they are disturbed.

Almost any business in the world can be undertaken redemptively, partly because each is concerned with persons and there are always numerous personal contacts in any business. What we have a right to expect now is the emergence of creative thinking about the application of lay religion to areas of common life. This is our most important twentieth-century frontier. Some people are already giving their thought to the development of this frontier and new ideas are appearing in heartening numbers. One of the most successful of the committees at the

World Council of Churches in 1948 was that devoted to the work of the layman, and some indication of its vigor may be gleaned from the pages of *Man's Disorder and God's Design*. Reports of new life in the work of lay men and women came from nearly every section of Christendom. The Apostolate of the Laity was a familiar phrase. In subsequent meetings in the summer of 1949, notably at the World Christian Youth Commission in Lausanne, there was equal emphasis on lay religion and on "youth in industry." The Study Department of the World Council of Churches, at Oxford, dealt with "the evangelization of man in modern mass society."

If enough able minds combine in creative thinking today we may see startlingly novel results. We may see something comparable to the release of power when the atom is split. That kind of work does not do itself. It comes only by the laborious imagination of many. The lay movement at the middle of our confused century is part of the evidence of a new reformation, because it is beginning to demonstrate some of this laborious imagination.

CHAPTER V

The Growth of Redemptive Societies

Two people, three people, ten people may be in living touch
with one another through Him who underlies their separate
lives. This is an astounding experience, which I can only
describe but cannot explain in the language of science.

THOMAS KELLY

OFTEN, in the recent past, those who have sought to
ally themselves with a religious movement to which
they could give themselves fully have been faced with a
hard and cruel choice. On the one hand, they could find
plenty of dull and conventional churches with sound
theology, but with little imagination in the development
of new ways of meeting human need. On the other hand,
they could find those with vigor and freshness of approach,
but too often these groups gave the impression of being
unintelligent fanatics so far as fundamental faith is concerned. The choice between dull orthodoxy and fanatical
freshness is indeed a hard choice and we cannot blame
many seekers for rejecting both. The "First Church" on
the corner and the Pentecostal group in the store front are
equally uninviting, though for different reasons. The one
is correct and dead while the other is alive, but intel-
lectually unsound.

97

One of the really wonderful facts of our day is that there is springing up spontaneously, in various areas, something that is genuinely a third alternative. A third way is emerging which can give seekers a better choice than either sound dullness or imaginative heresy. There is an unorganized movement which is marked by the emergence of Christian fellowships which are in line with the vigorous theological thinking described in Chapter III and which have found new ways of breaking the crust of apathetic respectability. Sometimes this is called the "Cell Movement," but the phrase is not a particularly happy one and will not be used, for the most part, in this chapter. The essence of the new development is the discovery or rediscovery of the explosive power that lies in a really committed group who seek to witness *together* to the life and reality of the Living Christ.

The best known of all the contemporary redemptive fellowships is the Iona Community, which has been described in many books[1] and which has inspired great numbers of similar experiments in other parts of the earth. On the tiny island of the Inner Hebrides, forty miles west of the Scottish mainland, a group of artisans and clergymen, who are members of the Church of Scotland, live together each summer and create a fellowship of work and study. They try to recover something of a sense of the wholeness of life by rebuilding the ancient ruined buildings of the famous Iona Abbey with their own hands, but their interests do not center on the island. What really concerns them

[1] One of the best interpretations of the basic idea of Iona is *We Shall Rebuild* by George MacLeod.

is the renewal of the entire life of the Scottish nation, the recovery of its faith and the enkindling of its youth. During the winter months all of the members work at their common tasks and try to build little Ionas in their mainland communities, often in the form of community centers. Their conception of real religion is that of Ezekiel who saw in a parable a stream rising underneath the altar in the Holy City and, instead of *staying* there, flowing out to water the parched secular earth outside. This likewise was the conception of Columba and his helpers who first used the tiny island and its abbey as a point of departure and a center of operations in the sixth century of our era. Far from separating themselves from common life, the members of the community are seeking identification with common life at every point. As a symbol of this, the bread used in Holy Communion at Iona is a loaf of ordinary rough Scottish bread, and when the service in the Abbey is over, the remainder of the loaf appears on the dinner table in the community house.

The most remarkable feature of the modern Iona community is not in its own activity, but in its extraordinary fertility. Other Ionas are springing up in the most surprising places and reproducing the idea. The many visitors who go to the island each summer and share for a few days in the total life usually leave with a new inspiration which seems quite out of proportion to the minuteness of the experiment. Among the American communities which likewise are devoted to the development of redemptive fellowships are Kirkridge, near Bangor, Pennsylvania, and Parishfield, north of Ann Arbor, Michigan. Pendle Hill at

Wallingford, Pennsylvania, and Quaker Hill, at Richmond, Indiana, belong to the same essential tradition though each center has its own unique features, Pendle Hill being more largely educational than others.

The most numerous of modern fellowships of this kind have appeared in colleges and so widespread are they that there is hardly an institution of higher education in the United States without at least one such group. The usual procedure is for three or four students to start together in their practice of daily or weekly devotion, to add concerned persons to them until they reach ten or twelve and divide into two. One college has eleven such fellowships and many have three or four. The meetings are given over to prayer, corporate silence, Bible reading, the sharing of problems and often the planning of some work project. Frequently it is necessary to hold the regular meetings at some unconventional hour, such as six o'clock in the morning, in order for the attenders to be free from competing claims upon time. All of these accept a voluntary discipline, usually one of their own making, and, therefore, exhibiting great variety.

The student movements based on the conception of substituting concerned and unapologetic fellowships for the mass movements heretofore so familiar, and often so ineffective in total impact, are so numerous that it is impracticable to list them all. If we should try we should be sure to miss some of them. Ours is, in this regard, at least similar to the time when Puritanism was at its height, and when there were many different movements with different names, but all belonging to one spiritual ground swell, the wave of the seventeenth century. In the wave of the present we also find a score of names and sometimes they are not conscious of mutual inspiration, but actually all are influenced by the same climate of opinion. All that we can profitably do, as we try to demonstrate signs of hope, is to point to characteristic examples on different levels.

A striking movement in the South, particularly among Southern Baptists, is called "The Master's Minority." This name is adopted in order to accentuate the idea that those who stand openly for a vital Christianity on their respective campuses will not be in the main secular stream. It recognizes the fact that the major mood of most universities, in the South or anywhere else, is pagan, and that the concerned Christians will require a certain amount of courage to declare their position and be true to it. The organization is an effort to buttress the minority, to encourage its members to be unapologetic in their daily witness and to be frankly evangelistic in trying to advance the Christian Campaign.

The Master's Minority Movement came into being recently through the vision of Frank H. Leavell of Nashville to whom the idea first came in 1926. Since that time the movement has spread all over the South and its story has now been told in a book.[2] One of the most effective features of this movement is the frank use of the vow or covenant which, to some, has seemed a relic of a bygone age, but which has proved to be most effective. The Covenant helps the ordinary young person to go beyond the vague re-

[2] *The Master's Minority*, by Frank H. Leavell (Nashville: Broadman Press, 1949).

ligiosity which has often seemed the height of "spirituality" and gives concrete substance to the endeavor which is undertaken. The young person who signs this pledge signs something definite and knows what he signs. Then he either keeps it or doesn't. Naturally not all keep it, but the experience is that the very act of signing is beneficent for most. It is like making a public witness and thus adding a powerful incentive. This is particularly true of those who have a high sense of honor about their signatures and being trustworthy in regard to promises. Many of us might criticize the choice of items in the eight point Covenant of the Minority members, but we are not likely to doubt the wisdom of the method unless we subscribe unconsciously to the angelic fallacy and suppose that we are too strong to need outward helps.

The Lutheran Student Movement accepts gladly the idea of minority groups and explains carefully the nature of a group formed in this spirit. "This 'little flock' " they say, "is not a *pressure* group but a *prayer* group. Those comprising this group may be called God's 'remembrancers.' " Some of these make small wooden crosses which they give to one another to carry with their coins as personal reminders.

The Northern Baptists, like their Southern brethren and like the young Lutherans, have caught the growing idea and have produced their "Discipleship Plan." Unsatisfied with the old-fashioned type of youth program, they, starting with a group of twelve, and going on to a national group of seventy, finally launched, at Green Lake, Wisconsin, in 1944, a movement made up of five hundred committed young people. Since its inception the movement has spread contagiously, partly because its demands on young people are great. The entire emphasis is on full life commitment, whatever the particular vocation may be, and the seriousness of the enterprise is indicated by the fact so many have registered their discipleship in daily living and service. Discipleship has been the motivating spirit behind many service projects, caravans, evangelists' teams and interne service. In all this we are a long way from the kind of religious experience which involves chiefly attending a meeting, shaking someone's hand and going home without any specific guidance as to particular steps to be taken. The resultant fellowships are intense in their fundamental nature because of the discipleship idea, which necessarily makes membership functional rather than nominal. The pledge is:

I will live my life under God for others rather than for myself; for the advancement of the kingdom of God rather than for my personal success.

I will do my utmost by prayer, investigation, meditation, and service, to avoid drifting in my work in life, and to seek out the place and form of work where I can become of the largest use to the kingdom of God.

As I find my place of largest usefulness, I will prepare for it and follow it, under the leadership of Jesus Christ, wheresoever it takes me, cost what it may.

The Work Camp idea is an important part of the entire Christian campaign in this generation and has now spread in a remarkable way. Though the summer work camps planned primarily for college students were first nurtured by the American Friends Service Committee, and though the camps under this committee's sponsorship are still numerous, the idea has spread to many denominations and to many countries. The idea recently embodied in summer projects was inspired partly by the conceptions of Pierre Ceresole and the principles back of the ISVP (International Volunteers for Peace Service), and was given its first serious trial in America during the summer of 1934 in western Pennsylvania. From the beginning the camps included, or were meant to include, at least the following: (1) A service project designed to meet a specific human need including, when possible, physical labor. (2) No payment of salaries to campers for work done, but, instead, the requirement that each participant should pay his own way in so far as he might be able. (3) Some guidance in the experience of meditation and prayer, including adequate provision for daily worship.

At first the camps were summer projects only, but more recently some year-round work camps have been organized. An important development has been the growing connection with mental hospitals where the young campers come into direct and eye-opening contact with some of the strongest evidences of contemporary cultural decay. The concentration on such work arose partly from the experience of men of the Civilian Public Service Camps during the war who engaged in the demanding yet unpaid work of orderlies and helpers in several mental hospitals and consequently came away with a keen sense of how inadequate is our general handling of the problem of mental illness. Another development of the work camp idea has led to the formation of American-supported camps abroad, particularly in Germany. Some of these have been under denominational sponsorship and some have been sponsored by Church World Service.

There is abundant evidence that this sort of Christian expression is making a remarkable difference in the lives of thousands of young people and for most of them it is strictly new. Most of those so affected are young people who heretofore have known either no religion or a merely conventional religion in which they were spectators rather than participators. The glory comes with the reality of sharing in both worship and work. Nowhere has this creative effect been more evident than in the Interseminary Movement, an effort not only to build up an ecumenical consciousness in those attending the various theological seminaries of the different denominations, but also to deepen the spiritual experience of those who are being trained to minister to others. It is recognized that it is impossible for a person to give what he does not have, and the Interseminary Movement is using the cell technique to facilitate growth in genuine Christian experience. The preparation which came in this way helped to make the Interseminary Conference which convened at Oxford, Ohio, in June, 1947, not merely another conference, but a revolutionary time in the lives of most of the six hundred young people who attended. Something of the same creative effect was evident in the National Student Christian Conference of twelve hundred students, which ended at Lawrence, Kansas, on New Year's Day, 1949. It was smaller than many previous gatherings, but much more effective.

The intensive groups which began in the colleges are now appearing in ordinary parish churches and are, in some instances, proving to be the means of genuine reformation. The method is not merely that of geographical units or colonies within the church membership, which are themselves helpful, but rather the encouragement of groups of persons, irrespective of location, who are willing to be unapologetically Christian and to share their Christian experience with one another in a disciplined way. The result is that hundreds now know the joys of vocal prayer and of group silence who, though church members for years, had never known these at all nor had any idea that they were missing anything. It is a wonderful thing to see people who have for years been faithful church members or even attenders suddenly begin to experience a new level of life and to be emancipated by it. Perhaps the one local church which has explored this method most fully is Calvary Church in New York where the influence of Samuel Shoemaker is felt continually in this direction.

The new disciplined fellowships spring up in the most unlikely places. One meets three times a week in an otherwise unoccupied train on Track 13 of Grand Central Station in New York. The organizer is a Negro porter, Redcap Number 42, whose group welcomes strangers at 11:55 on Mondays, Wednesdays, and Fridays. A group having many of the characteristics already described, meets in the stricken city of Cologne, most of its members being Roman Catholics. Though there has been formed no national organization of the movement, all efforts in this direction having been wisely resisted, Lane Hall, Ann Arbor, Michigan, has been an unofficial clearing house for ideas and the fifth National Cell Conference was held at Earlham College in October, 1949. Abingdon-Cokesbury Press has published a booklet by Harvey Seifert called *Fellowships of Concern.*

Though many of these signs of new life are strictly new in the sense that they were not even contemplated in their present form a generation ago, there is a deep sense in which they are not new at all, but rather a discovery of something that is very old and something that has never been wholly lost. In essence they represent a recovery of the original Christian Way. The center of Christ's strategy was the formation of a fellowship of such intensity that it could carry on when his earthly existence should be ended. Instead of writing a book, he built a cell of twelve common men and believed that the fertility of their fellowship would be sufficient to maintain the movement. Christ spent a great deal of his active ministry, not in what we should call public work, but in the intense preparation of his Society of Witnesses which became the early Christian Church and which, against terrible odds, won in the ancient world. They were the salt that could save the world from corruption and if they should lose their effectiveness nothing else would suffice, he said.

S. D. Gordon used to move great audiences with an imaginary conversation between Christ and the Angel Gabriel in heaven. Christ, after leaving his earthly career, returned to heaven and told Gabriel of the whole redemptive enterprise. He told of his birth, baptism, ministry, resurrection and ascension, but since this was obviously not the completion of the narrative, Gabriel asked him what provision he had made for the continuation of the work and what assurance he had that it would be perpetuated. Jesus answered simply that he had chosen twelve men to whom as a group he had committed the continuation of his earthly life and ministry. "And what if they should fail you?" asked the angel. To this Christ's only reply was, "I have no other plan."

The history of Christianity has been that of the emergence of truly redemptive fellowships, the Order of the Salt, and their eventual decay, as religion has become a dull and almost meaningless affair or the professional concern of a priestly group. But the salt has never lost its savor so badly that renewal was impossible. The situation has been like that of the famous Dismal Swamp, in which fires break out during the hot dry months because, in spite of the long winter rains, the deep fires of the peat bogs are never wholly extinguished.

The way in which the dynamic power resident in a committed group has been rediscovered in unlikely places and at unlikely times is one of the most hopeful features of our checkered human history. It is the story of the Franciscans, of the Lollards, of the Brethren of the Common Life, of the Society of Jesus, of the early Quakers, of the Methodist Class Meeting. The power resident in Robert Barclay and his fellow prisoners as they lay, for conscience' sake, in Aberdeen prison in the long winter of 1676-1677, was so great that they, though few, became some of the crucial factors in bringing to an end religious persecution in Great Britain. Forty or fifty such men who combine the power of religious commitment with the power of group solidarity are almost unbeatable; they often do far more for mankind than is accomplished by a thousand men of lukewarm convictions, secular loyalties and no real solidarity. D. L. Moody is reported to have said that the world has yet to see what can be accomplished by twelve truly dedicated men. Not even the Twelve were that.

Among the pioneers of our contemporary revival of stress on the redemptive power resident in devoted though small groups, the late Henry Hodgkin was more influential than is generally realized. As an English physician, as a missionary in China and as the first Director of Pendle Hill, he started developments which have been taken up by others, but he also left his most infectious ideas in print. The chief volumes which give his theory of how the world is to be remade and mankind brought into the life which is life indeed are *Lay Religion* and *The Christian Revolution*. Both have long been out of print, but might profitably be reissued. In *The Christian Revolution* which Dr. Hodgkin dedicated to his household, "colleagues in trying to make one little spot where love is supreme and where the Christian Revolution can begin," he outlined his hope of world renewal by the formation of islands in the pagan sea. Slowly the islands grow and proliferate as occurs when a continent emerges from the ocean. This is how Christianity won in the Graeco-Roman world and it is the way, Dr. Hodgkin thought, that we shall win in our time, if we win at all. He believed that Christian experiments can be infectious just as diseases are. The growth of movements such as he described have, in the last two decades, been partial verifications of his faith.

Another influential pioneer in the same field has been Thomas Kelly whose *A Testament of Devotion* has been one of the most prized religious books of our generation. To occupy the chair at Earlham which he occupied for many years is to me a searching experience and also a great encouragement. Thomas Kelly did not know that the essays collected in the well-known devotional volume would be published as a book, for he was cut off in the midst of life, but some of the young men whom he had formed into an intense fellowship have continued to demonstrate the power which this prayer group at Haverford generated or released. Thomas Kelly's "Holy Obedience" is one of the best statements of the real secret of Christian power.

Because the sort of thing for which Thomas Kelly stood is hard to put into words, misunderstanding is easily possible. The unguarded reader is apt to think that he is being introduced to something esoteric and queer, whereas it is the simple experience at the heart of Christian discipleship which is, by its very nature, *group* discipleship. What we are trying to describe is what ought to be a normal experience, something genuinely indigenous to Christianity, and certainly nothing cultish. The Christian gospel affirms the absolute and transcendent worth of the individual soul, but in practice it is a group experience and never mere solitariness. A man may, of course, be awakened when alone, but, if his Christian conviction is real, it will drive him to form or support a group. As was indicated in Chapter II, the social aspects of Christianity are not incidental features or resultants, but belong to its essential nature. This may be part of the deep significance of Christ's enigmatical remark about John the Baptist. John was a voice crying the wilderness, but Christ made a Society of Witnesses. John had a few followers, but nothing comparable to the Twelve.[3] John left an idea, but Christ left a living and therefore an enduring fellowship. "Verily I say unto you," said Christ, "Among them that are born of women there hath not arisen a greater than John the Baptist; notwithstanding he that is least in the kingdom of heaven is greater than he."[4] If our understanding of the gospel is correct, this paradox is not really difficult to understand. *Individual greatness is no match for humble togetherness.*

We can hardly express the Christian idea which is catching on in so many places today without using the word "fellowship," but the word is ambiguous. Too often it connotes the superficial conviviality which is so marked in secular societies, from luncheon clubs to reunions of the Brown family. If it is conviviality that will save the world we need not worry about the fate of civilization for we have plenty of that medicine. There is much apparent fellowship in the conventional cocktail party, but it is doubtful if this sort of fellowship is of much healing value when one's child lies desperately ill. What then, do we

3 Acts 19:3.
4 Matthew 11:11.

mean, in Christian terms, when we speak today of a fellowship that is redemptive and part of Christ's plan of campaign in which we can share.

One good way to make the meaning of this deeper fellowship clear is to contrast it with the once popular discussion group. Once the discussion group seemed a great discovery and it became the central feature of student religious gatherings. It seemed wonderful because it was so much better than the mere passive listening to lectures. But we realize today that there is something as far beyond the discussion group as it was beyond the lecture. This new emphasis is not upon argument *about* God, but obedience *to* God. We realize that the discussion group may not be really religious in essence, even if it is devoted to religious questions, and may be actually *sacrilegious*. Discussion is a valuable human experience, but it is the beginning rather than the end, and it does not really belong to the same universe of discourse as does personal dedication. The teleological argument is interesting, but it would be a poor thing to live by, whereas personal commitment in which I make the great gamble and decide to be "Christ's Man" is something powerful to live by. *In so far as we have really gone forward in creative Christian minorities in the midst of the world civil war, that advancement may be conveniently symbolized by the movement from discussion to commitment.* Often, today, the center of spiritual power on a college campus is found, not in an old-fashioned bull session, but in a group who share every day in Holy communion. The movement is from argument to prayer.

The committed groups, whose fellowship differs in kind from the conviviality of the fraternities and clubs, find that they are driven, in nearly all instances, to the acceptance of voluntary discipline. The majority may still be satisfied with the now outmoded philosophy of self-expression, but the creative minorities have usually discovered the power which discipline releases and the freedom which it makes possible. It is easy for me to see that the disciplined pianist is far more free in his movements than I am; he is free to put his fingers on the right keys at the right time and I am not. The new movement we are noting as an evidence of hope in a century of storm accepts this conclusion, not only for art and music, but likewise for the life of the spirit.

Nearly all the new cells which arise begin very early to work out a group discipline. They believe that they must be severe with themselves at crucial points, especially in the right use of time and money, which is capitalized time. They seek no trivial or Puritanical restrictions like the giving up of meat on Fridays in order to eat excellent fish instead, but rather those items of discipline which may reasonably be expected to guide human energies into more productive channels. The usual minimum discipline of almost any truly concerned group includes absolute regularity in attendance at public worship, absolute regularity in private devotional practices such as the "plotted day" and a strict sense of stewardship of money in the light of human suffering. In a number of conferences, where this general principle is accepted, the attenders follow the practice of complete silence between the close of the evening session and breakfast the following morning.

The new groups who undertake voluntary discipline with a sense of joyous release are heartened by the fact that discipline has, at various periods of history, been a major secret of power on the part of otherwise very ordinary people. One of the most amazing stories of success and one that we can ponder with profit is that of Ignatius Loyola in his formation of the Society of Jesus in 1540.

As we study this remarkable story we soon realize that his insistence in the necessity of discipline was not a detail, but central to the idea. He had been a soldier and he was greatly influenced by the campaign to rid Spain of the infidels. In this mood, he saw the Christian life as a campaign under a Captain and Christ was appealing, he thought, for volunteers. Naturally, it seemed to him, those who volunteer in a campaign must be toughened and learn to overcome softness. For this purpose he originated *The Spiritual Exercises* which have constituted for four hundred years one of the chief secrets of Jesuit power.

The *Directory to the Spiritual Exercises* of Ignatius Loyola, given at Rome, *1599,* begins:

Among the instruments which God of his goodness and clemency has vouchsafed to give to our Society for the furtherance both of our own and our neighbor's salvation and perfection, the Spiritual Exercises stand in the front rank.

Later it says:

Lastly, there is the experience of the great and well-nigh incredible benefit which is wont to follow upon the use of these Exercises. For in the first place very many of ours, especially in early days, received in this way the spirit of their vocation, so that it might be truly said that it was by means of the Exercises that our Society came together in the beginning and afterward received its increase.

The Jesuit order ought not to be copied now because it is sectarian rather than ecumenical or truly catholic in its aim, and because it is limited in membership to an abnormal group of men without the joys and sorrows of parenthood or ordinary responsibilities in ordinary life. What we seek and what we are beginning to see in small, but infectious experiments, is disciplined groups devoted to the whole redemptive purpose of Christ rather than the aggrandizement of one human institution, and also groups made up of men and women immersed in ordinary life with family burdens and with common secular jobs in the world. One of the greatest calamities of history was the failure of the Franciscan Third Order which was envisioned as an experiment in disciplined living, not for monks and nuns, or even for priests, but for mothers and fathers and workers of the secular world. What is called a Third Order still exists, but it is a far cry from this revolutionary conception of the poor little man of Assisi, whose successors are now as respectable as he was dangerous.

The real problem of discipline is the problem of its application to common life. It is a relatively simple matter to apply the principle of disciplined existence to the routine of a monastery or even to the temporary retirement of an Ashram or conference, but it is not a simple thing to apply it to the life of families with the variety of demands and the continual crises which family life entails. Yet this is the point at which success is most important and where emphasis must be placed. Something of this was achieved

by early Methodists and is the factor which helps to explain
the rapid and extraordinary success of the Wesleyan Movement. The very name "Methodist" is, of course, a nick-
name for a disciplined person and the early meetings at
Oxford were different from others of the time because
they were made up of disciplined men. What several groups
are essaying today is not some novelty, but the recovery
and reapplication of a principle already native to their
tradition, though long neglected. The problem is to avoid
the trivial, the merely negative and the merely traditional
items of discipline, in order to accentuate instead items
which are as directly applicable to the development of
Christian sensitivity as the finger exercises of the violinist
are applicable to his artistry in the reproduction of great
compositions.

Many of the efforts to recover discipline in our time are
unpublicized and therefore quite unknown. One man, for
example, has produced his own rule which he has no
thought of publishing or advertising, though he has printed
a little flier which he sometimes distributes privately. In
it he says, "My discipline is personal. I will not seek to talk
about it or organize it. I will be content to appeal to others
by handing them this folder in the hope that they will
consider it personally and practice it the same way. No
census is to be taken or tally to be kept." This particular
seeker after the disciplined Christian life has constructed
seven pointed questions which he asks himself every week,
concentrating on a different one of the seven on each day
of the week and thus engaging in self-examination. He
believes, with Socrates, that the unexamined life is not

worth living. Such a man is really part of a growing, but largely anonymous fellowship of which the world has not yet, for the most part, become aware.

In the Episcopal Church there are small societies, especially among students, who undertake to participate in Holy Communion every day and make a pledge to that effect. One group in this church has distributed a small flier called "My Bounden Duty,"[5] which includes the following pledge:

As a follower of Christ and as a co-worker with Him, I will make an earnest effort with God's help:

I. *To Worship God Every Sunday in His Church.*
This will include receiving the Holy Communion regularly after I have made careful preparation by self-examination, penitence, and prayer.

II. *To Pray Daily.* The goal toward which I aim will include morning prayers of praise, self-dedication, and petition; evening prayers of penitence, thanksgiving, and intercession; and grace at meals.

III. *To Set Aside a Definite Amount of Time Each Day for Devotional Reading.* The book I will use most often is the Bible with the assistance of such devotional manuals as *Forward: Youth Edition* and The Book of Common Prayer. I will read slowly to find a message for myself. I shall endeavor to develop a regular schedule. For further devotional reading I will consult my pastor.

IV. *To Give a Definite Portion of Time and Money to the Life and Work of the Whole Church.* This calls for determined effort on my part: to help others to find Christ in the Church; to take an active part in parish work; and to make a stated weekly contribution.

[5] Copies may be secured from The National Council, 281 Fourth Avenue, New York 10, New York.

Every thoughtful person who considers this movement in the direction of disciplined Christian fellowships realizes immediately that there are dangers in it. One of the greatest dangers is that of spiritual snobbery. Will not these groups, it is often asked, tend to become circles of men and women who feel that they have arrived, and thereby constitute a spiritual élite? This is a real and present danger and was even a danger in New Testament times. The enemies of George Fox accused him of having such convictions about the movement which he helped to originate while the charge has often been leveled at Jesuits and other groups which make strong demands.

There are two important things to say about this potential criticism. First we must understand that every good thing has dangers and difficulties and not make the mistake of giving up a project merely because it has difficulties. The question is not whether it is dangerous, but whether the alternative is *more dangerous*. There are dangers in the creation of disciplined groups, but perhaps there are even greater dangers in the *failure* to have disciplined groups, especially the awful danger of continued lethargy, of spectator religion and of vague religiosity which is harder to overcome than is frank paganism.

The other important thing to say about this obvious criticism is that those most concerned with the movement, if it is a movement, are deeply aware of the danger and try to face it frankly. What nearly all discover is that the new intensity does not make men feel good, but makes them more keenly aware that they are not good. The people who feel virtuous are not the deeply concerned, but rather, as a terrible report in the *Ladies' Home Journal* showed, the rank and file of the citizens. If this report is correct the majority are so complacent as to believe that they are really living up to the law of Christian love. In actual practice, membership in a truly concerned society, far from accentuating this loathsome self-righteousness, helps to overcome it.

The general situation is made better and the worst dangers partially avoided by the wide acceptance of the theological emphasis analyzed in Chapter III. Those who have been deeply influenced by the new evangelicalism, particularly in its insistence on the indigenous and chronic nature of human sin, are not really likely to be easily persuaded that they belong to a fellowship of saints. They may have superior concern, but they know they lack superior virtue.

A second obvious danger is that of cliquishness. Those who make up dynamic fellowships may be conscious that, whatever they do, they do as sinners and yet in practice form themselves into right little, tight little bodies, largely enjoying their own group life and so satisfied by it that they do not bother much with the outside world. This is particularly true of those who have a strongly mystical approach to religion. It is easy for them to develop their jargon, to have their own little roster of saints, to live through most of the year pining for the time when their special camp opens again in the summer and they can again be surrounded by the congenial persons who "belong" and who speak the same language. Such an existence is so much more comfortable than is that of the rough and tumble world of hard-hearted men and women who have never even heard the name of the revered camp leader and who do not respond appropriately to the verbal stimuli that are so effective in the small clique.

The danger just mentioned has been accentuated by the fact that some adherents of small group movements have been mentally unbalanced, without any consciousness that this is the case. There is a tendency in some groups to attract those who are personally maladjusted and some-times the leaders are obviously suffering from aberrations themselves. This is shown whenever the members revel in eccentricity. Our only safety lies in a frank awareness of the danger, in a strong insistence on normal healthy living, such as was made constantly by the late Rufus Jones in all his interpretations of mysticism and, above all, in a vig-orous program of practical work in the world. The mem-bers of the Iona Community are largely saved from cliqu-ishness by the hard manual labor in which they engage, ministers working shoulder to shoulder with carpenters, and by the expectation of practical community work in ordinary villages and cities during the bulk of the year.

Any disciplined society which makes its own meetings or conferences its climactic experience is almost sure to demonstrate the very evils which its critics expect. Safety lies in the inauguration of a pattern of rhythm by which men oscillate between periods of intense concentration and periods of difficult or lonely human service, and the periods of service ought to be longer than are the periods of group concentration. Mere work becomes ineffective, because the inspiration for it dies, and mere conferencing becomes self-indulgent. Eventually the self-regarding group comes to resemble the Dead Sea, because it has no outlet to keep the water clean and pure.

Christ warned specifically against this danger, his warning appearing in the incident called the transfiguration. He took with him the most intense of early Christian fellowships, the inner circle of the disciples. They profited by it, but the difficulty was that they liked it so well that they wanted to stay permanently. They were like some of our young people who become "work camp tramps," going from camp to camp, but unable to throw themselves into some productive task in common life where the inspiration supposedly gained in camp can be put into effective practice. Christ's message to all such, as it was to Peter, James and John, is that they must leave the mountain and take their turn on the plain. I heard a strong sermon on this very theme at Iona in the summer of 1948.

A temptation which comes to most fellowships when they discover the power and joy of commitment is to draw away, almost unconsciously, from the church. As they gather for Bible study or prayer or mutual witness they enjoy their own fellowship so much better than that of the parish church that they virtually secede from it altogether. There is a strong tendency to make men feel satisfied without a vital church connection. Some specialized groups, for example, actually meet at eleven o'clock on Sunday morning, precisely at the time when most parish church services are held. If this is carried on long, the group tends to become another sect and there is very little gain in that direction, so far as the entire Christian cause is concerned.

Comparative safety lies in a strong insistence on the necessity of working with the church and *within* the church, however imperfect it may be. We must resist the temptations of perfectionism by which we so love the ideal which we have constructed in our own imaginations that we cannot bear the poor human institution with which most people have to work if they work at all. Too often, in the past, vigorous new movements have been separated from the parent body with the result that both lose, since the revolutionary group becomes a mere sect, a leaven without a lump, while the parent body misses the infectious influence which the group should have continued to impart. We can be wonderfully thankful for the new life springing up in the general deadness of our day, but we must plead with its representatives to seek to remain firmly within the church and revolutionize it *from the inside*.

A third danger is the greatest of all and calls for a particular warning. This is the danger, which comes so easily in connection with strong or attractive personalities. Some otherwise wonderful movements in the modern world are deeply spoiled by the willingness of leaders or organizers to receive adulation from followers. Cultishness is always bad. The one certain test that a movement has become a cult lies in the presence or absence of disciples of the group leader. If a man welcomes or even permits personal disciples he is already suspect. Only One who ever lived was good enough to have disciples. More religious leaders are ruined by the flattery of admirers than by any other single factor. The real cure is a double one: a devotion to Christ so genuine that a man sees himself in his right size, and a lively sense of humor.

Great as are the dangers of the new life that is emerging, the alternative dangers are worse. The really frightening danger is not that of the lunatic fringe, which always surrounds any new movement, but rather the prospect that we shall die on our feet, that our Christianity shall continue to be merely the conventional religion of the respectable people of those parts of the world most influenced by European culture. Our alarming problem is not that of the overzealousness of disciplined groups, but the lethargy of the common churchmen who are satisfied with a clergyman's religion which expresses itself one hour a week. The great Professor Whitehead moved many by his demonstration that, by the very nature of the world order, there are only two possibilities open to mankind and never three. *There is no middle road.* If we are not advancing we are already retreating. The one thing we can *never* do is stand still, hold our own and conserve our resources. The moment we try to do that we are already in retreat and decline. The only way by which we can avoid calamity is to take the offensive.

Perhaps the greatest sign of hope in our perplexing age is the fact that, on so many different sectors, the Christian army is taking the offensive and moving forward. Ours is still a young religion. Other movements have started and have died since the Order of the Salt was founded in Galilee more than nineteen hundred years ago. This Order has survived the fall of Rome and the Dark Ages and the

Renaissance and the Reformation and the Industrial Revolution and it *is* surviving in the century of the Great Civil War. It is a rational conclusion, as well as a Christian hope, that ten thousand years from now, *if there are then any men at all on this planet, and if we make our witness now as we ought in order to survive through the critical years just ahead,* the Christian society will still be vigorous and will still continue the redemptive work begun by Christ. The men of that distant time will look back upon our confused century with wonder, and they will think of us as living near the beginning of the Christian Movement. They will be right. We are living, as Professor Latourette has so brilliantly said, "in the early days of the Christian Church." Some day even the terrible divisions of Christendom will be overcome because all of us, Roman and non-Roman alike, will have passed beyond our present sectarianism to the basic Christianity of personal and group commitment to One Lord.

It is almost certain that our descendants will, in future centuries, look back upon the middle of the twentieth century with pity and terror. They will know something of the narrowness of the margin by which our survival is accomplished, but they, as they sense our dangers, may even have a tinge of envy. They may become convinced that these early days of storm, the first decade of the Hiroshima age, were great and exciting days in which to live, both because of the dramatic character of the events and because of the vigor of new ideas. The major ideas which are creative of the future now will not seem quaint because

they are really perennial, though they must be rediscovered.

As we think now of the beginnings of the Christian
Church, we often suppose it would have been wonderful to
be alive then. It would have been exciting to be early
Christians with all their dangers and with all their hopes.
But we need not pine, for we *are* early Christians. We are
living in the early days of the Christian Church!